SAP PRESS Books: Always on hand

Print or e-book, Kindle or iPad, workplace or airplane: Choose where and how to read your SAP PRESS books! You can now get all our titles as e-books, too:

- By download and online access
- For all popular devices
- And, of course, DRM-free

Convinced? Then go to www.sap-press.com and get your e-book today.

Document Management with SAP® DMS

SAP PRESS is a joint initiative of SAP and Galileo Press. The know-how offered by SAP specialists combined with the expertise of the Galileo Press publishing house offers the reader expert books in the field. SAP PRESS features first-hand information and expert advice, and provides useful skills for professional decision-making.

SAP PRESS offers a variety of books on technical and business-related topics for the SAP user. For further information, please visit our website: *www.sap-press.com*.

Hanneke Raap
SAP Product Lifecycle Management
2013, approx. 850 pp., hardcover
ISBN 978-1-59229-418-3

Stefan Glatzmaier and Michael Sokollek
Project Portfolio Management with SAP RPM and cProjects
2008, 355 pp., hardcover
ISBN 978-1-59229-224-0

Gerd Hartmann and Ulrich Schmidt
Product Lifecycle Management with SAP
2005, 617 pp., hardcover
ISBN 978-1-59229-036-9

Eric Stajda

Document Management with SAP® DMS

Bonn • Boston

Galileo Press is named after the Italian physicist, mathematician, and philosopher Galileo Galilei (1564–1642). He is known as one of the founders of modern science and an advocate of our contemporary, heliocentric worldview. His words *Eppur si muove* (And yet it moves) have become legendary. The Galileo Press logo depicts Jupiter orbited by the four Galilean moons, which were discovered by Galileo in 1610.

Editor Katy Spencer
Copyeditor Julie McNamee
Cover Design Graham Geary
Photo Credit iStockphoto.com/368187/Joss
Layout Design Vera Brauner
Production Graham Geary
Typesetting Publishers' Design and Production Services, Inc.
Printed and bound in the United States of America, on paper from sustainable sources

ISBN 978-1-59229-862-4

© 2013 by Galileo Press Inc., Boston (MA)

2nd edition 2013

Library of Congress Cataloging-in-Publication Data
Stajda, Eric.
 Document management with SAP DMS / Eric Stajda. — 2nd edition.
    pages cm
 ISBN 978-1-59229-862-4 — ISBN 1-59229-862-1 — ISBN 978-1-59229-863-1 — ISBN 978-1-59229-864-8 1. Business records—Data processing—Management. 2. Commercial documents—Data processing—Management. 3. Management information systems. 4. SAP ERP. I. Title.
 HF5736.S76 2013
 651.50285'53—dc23
                                                            2013011905

All rights reserved. Neither this publication nor any part of it may be copied or reproduced in any form or by any means or translated into another language, without the prior consent of Galileo Press GmbH, Rheinwerkallee 4, 53227 Bonn, Germany.

Galileo Press makes no warranties or representations with respect to the content hereof and specifically disclaims any implied warranties of merchantability or fitness for any particular purpose. Galileo Press assumes no responsibility for any errors that may appear in this publication.

"Galileo Press" and the Galileo Press logo are registered trademarks of Galileo Press GmbH, Bonn, Germany. SAP PRESS is an imprint of Galileo Press.

All of the screenshots and graphics reproduced in this book are subject to copyright © SAP AG, Dietmar-Hopp-Allee 16, 69190 Walldorf, Germany.

SAP, the SAP logo, ABAP, BAPI, Duet, mySAP.com, mySAP, SAP ArchiveLink, SAP EarlyWatch, SAP NetWeaver, SAP Business ByDesign, SAP BusinessObjects, SAP BusinessObjects Rapid Mart, SAP BusinessObjects Desktop Intelligence, SAP BusinessObjects Explorer, SAP Rapid Marts, SAP BusinessObjects Watchlist Security, SAP BusinessObjects Web Intelligence, SAP Crystal Reports, SAP GoingLive, SAP HANA, SAP MaxAttention, SAP MaxDB, SAP PartnerEdge, SAP R/2, SAP R/3, SAP R/3 Enterprise, SAP Strategic Enterprise Management (SAP SEM), SAP StreamWork, SAP Sybase Adaptive Server Enterprise (SAP Sybase ASE), SAP Sybase IQ, SAP xApps, SAPPHIRE NOW, and Xcelsius are registered or unregistered trademarks of SAP AG, Walldorf, Germany.

All other products mentioned in this book are registered or unregistered trademarks of their respective companies.

To my wife, Liz.
Thank you for keeping the tea cup filled,
and for letting me know that I could do it.

Contents at a Glance

1	Introduction	19
2	Questions to Answer before Starting Your SAP DMS Project	25
3	SAP DMS Step-by-Step Instructions	43
4	Configuring SAP DMS	83
5	Infrastructure Requirements	119
6	SAP DMS Security	135
7	Frontends to SAP DMS	155
8	SAP PLM 7.02 DMS Web UI	177
9	Integrating a CAD System to SAP DMS	209
10	Simple Document Approval Process using SAP Workflow	217
11	SAP DMS BAdIs and User Exits	235
12	Conclusion	253
A	Glossary	261
B	Review of Menu Items	265
C	The Author	271

Dear Reader,

In today's networked, highly regulated business world, it's essential that companies store their key documents effectively and securely. It's easy to lose your paper trail as business processes change and your workforce evolves. Without technical support, it's difficult—if not impossible—to keep track of every document across its lifecycle.

More than a digital filing cabinet, SAP DMS helps you organize and manage your documentation, supports business processes, and ensures that your documents meet compliance and regulatory requirements. Starting with an overview of what SAP DMS is, what its requirements are, and how to configure it, this book is now up to date for PLM 7.01 and 7.02. With all new information on Easy DMS, its integration with Microsoft, and an introduction to the new Web UI interface, I'm confident that you'll master all aspects of SAP DMS.

We at SAP PRESS are always eager to hear your opinion. What do you think about the second edition of *Document Management with SAP DMS*? As your comments and suggestions are our most useful tools to help us make our books the best they can be, we encourage you to visit our website at *www.sap-press.com* and share your feedback.

Thank you for purchasing a book from SAP PRESS!

Katy Spencer
Editor, SAP PRESS

Galileo Press
Boston, MA

katy.spencer@galileo-press.com
www.sap-press.com

Contents

1 Introduction ... 19

1.1	What Is SAP DMS?	19
1.2	Benefits of SAP DMS	20
1.3	SAP DMS Project Complexity	21
1.4	Resources Required for a Project	22
1.5	How to Use This Book	22
1.6	A Note on the Availability of SAP DMS	23
1.7	Summary	24

2 Questions to Answer before Starting Your SAP DMS Project ... 25

2.1	Defining Which Documents to Manage with SAP DMS	25
2.2	How Documents Fit Into the Overall Business Process	26
2.3	How to Search for Stored Documents	27
2.4	Define the Lifecycle of Documents	28
2.5	The Change Control Process	29
2.6	A Formal Approval Process	29
2.7	Identify Business Roles and Mapping	30
2.8	Security Requirements	30
2.9	Defining Which Type of Application Files to Store	31
2.10	Document Numbering	32
2.11	Change History Requirements	32
2.12	Versions and Revisions	33
2.13	Management of Content Versions	34
2.14	Searching and Maintenance in Multiple Languages	34
2.15	Full-Text Search Requirements	34
2.16	Stored Document Volume and Size	35
2.17	Locations for Document Creators versus Consumers	36
2.18	Document Retention Requirements	36
2.19	Conversion to Neutral Format for Long-Term Retention	37

Contents

	2.20	Interface with External Systems	37
	2.21	Data Migration Requirements	38
	2.22	Training	39
	2.23	Organizational Change Impact	39
	2.24	Summary	40

3   SAP DMS Step-by-Step Instructions 43

3.1		SAP DMS Transactions	43
3.2		Transaction CV01N: Creating a Document Information Record	44
	3.2.1	Execute Transaction CV01N (Create Document)	44
	3.2.2	Fill Out Relevant Fields on the Document Data Tab	45
	3.2.3	Add an Original File	46
	3.2.4	Check in an Original File	46
	3.2.5	Fill Out Attributes on the Addnl Data Tab	47
	3.2.6	Add a Language-Dependent Description	48
	3.2.7	Link the New Document to Another SAP Object	49
	3.2.8	Save the Document Information Record	52
3.3		Transaction CV02N: Changing a Document Information Record	52
	3.3.1	Execute Transaction CV02N (Change Document)	53
	3.3.2	Update the Description Field and Lab Office	54
	3.3.3	Change the Status of the Document Information Record	54
	3.3.4	Add Object Links	55
	3.3.5	Save the Document Information Record	55
	3.3.6	Create a New Version of the Document Information Record	55
	3.3.7	Check Out the Original File Associated with the New Version	56
	3.3.8	Check in the Original File after Changes	58
	3.3.9	Add Another Original File to the New Version	58
3.4		Transaction CV03N: Displaying a Document Information Record	59

	3.4.1	Display an Original File Associated with the Document Information Record	59
	3.4.2	Display the Status Network	59
	3.4.3	Review the Change History for the Document Information Record	61
	3.4.4	Check How Many Versions Are Available for a Document Information Record	62
3.5	Transaction CV04N: Searching for a Document Information Record		62
	3.5.1	Search for a Document Information Record by Document Type and User	64
	3.5.2	Search for a Document Information Record by Document Type and Classification Attributes	65
	3.5.3	Search for a Document Information Record by Object Link	66
	3.5.4	Search Long Text for a Document Information Record	67
	3.5.5	Full-Text Search	68
3.6	Additional SAP DMS Functionalities		68
	3.6.1	Copy a Document Information Record	69
	3.6.2	Delete a Document Information Record	69
	3.6.3	Show the Sequence of Sources	69
	3.6.4	Creating and Displaying the Document Hierarchy	69
	3.6.5	Display the Status Log	70
	3.6.6	Set and Display Revision Levels	70
	3.6.7	Execute a Document Where Used	70
	3.6.8	Create a Document Structure	71
	3.6.9	Copy an Original File to a Local Directory	71
	3.6.10	Reset Check-Out	71
3.7	Product Structure Browser		72
	3.7.1	Select the Focus of the Product Structure Browser	73
3.8	Classification Search		75
	3.8.1	Example Classification Search	75
3.9	Document Distribution		76
3.10	Internal Viewer		78
3.11	Summary		81

4 Configuring SAP DMS ... 83

- 4.1 Questions to Answer before Starting the Configuration ... 83
- 4.2 SAP DMS Configuration in the SAP IMG ... 84
- 4.3 Configuration Steps ... 84
- 4.4 Defining Number Ranges ... 84
- 4.5 Creating Document Types ... 86
  - 4.5.1 Configuration Location ... 88
  - 4.5.2 Configuration Example ... 88
  - 4.5.3 Configuration Steps ... 88
- 4.6 Defining Laboratories/Design Offices ... 103
- 4.7 Defining Revision Levels ... 104
- 4.8 Defining Workstation Applications ... 105
  - 4.8.1 Example Workstation Application: Microsoft Word ... 106
  - 4.8.2 Workstation Application Details ... 106
  - 4.8.3 Define Workstation Application in Network ... 108
  - 4.8.4 Define Templates for Original Files ... 110
  - 4.8.5 Set Up Microsoft Office Integration ... 110
- 4.9 Maintain a Default Entry for Frontend Type "PC" ... 111
- 4.10 Start Processing for Documents ... 112
- 4.11 Define Workstation Application for Thumbnails ... 114
- 4.12 Define Profile ... 115
- 4.13 Additional Configuration Items ... 117
- 4.14 Summary ... 117

5 Infrastructure Requirements ... 119

- 5.1 Content Server ... 119
  - 5.1.1 Content Server Requests ... 120
  - 5.1.2 Choosing Database- or File-Based Storage ... 121
  - 5.1.3 Key Transactions for the Content Server ... 121
  - 5.1.4 Content Server Quick Installation Guide ... 122
- 5.2 Cache Server ... 122
  - 5.2.1 Cache Size and Deletion ... 123
  - 5.2.2 Determining Path for Client Requests ... 124
  - 5.2.3 Key Transactions for the Cache Server ... 124

		5.2.4	Customizing for the Cache Server	124
	5.3	Index Server (TREX)		125
		5.3.1	Benefits of Full-Text Searching	125
		5.3.2	Executing a Full-Text Search	126
		5.3.3	Use of TREX and SAP PLM 7.01	126
	5.4	Conversion Server		127
		5.4.1	SAP Software's Part in the Conversion Process	127
		5.4.2	Sample Conversion Scripts and Tools	128
		5.4.3	Configuration of the Conversion Server	128
	5.5	Conversion with SAP Visual Enterprise Generator		129
	5.6	Developing Your Infrastructure Architecture		131
		5.6.1	Types of Users at Each Location	131
		5.6.2	Which Functionalities to Implement	131
		5.6.3	Wide Area Network Capability	132
	5.7	Summary		133

6 SAP DMS Security ... 135

	6.1	Defining Your Security Requirements		135
	6.2	Standard SAP DMS Authorization Objects		136
		6.2.1	Authorization Object C_DRAW_TCD: Activities for Documents	137
		6.2.2	Authorization Object C_DRAW_TCS: Status-Dependent Authorization	138
		6.2.3	Authorization Object C_DRAW_STA: Document Status	139
		6.2.4	Authorization Object C_DRAW_BGR: Authorization Group	140
		6.2.5	Authorization Object C_DRAD_OBJ: Object Link	141
		6.2.6	Authorization Object C_DRAW_DOK: Document Access	142
		6.2.7	Authorization Object C_DRZA_TCD: Activities for Recipient Lists	143
		6.2.8	Authorization Object C_DRZI_TCD: Distribution Order	144
	6.3	Additional Non-SAP DMS Authorization Objects		145

		6.3.1	Authorization Object C_TCLA_BKA: Authorization for Class Type	145
		6.3.2	Authorization Object C_KLAH_BKL: Authorization for Class Type	146
		6.3.3	Authorization Object C_STUE_BER: Bill of Material Maintenance	147
	6.4	Use of Access Control Lists		148
		6.4.1	Override of ACL via Authorization Object ACO_SUPER	151
	6.5	SAP PLM 7.01: Access Control Management		151
	6.6	Customer-Specific Authorization Checks		153
	6.7	Summary		154

7 Frontends to SAP DMS 155

	7.1	WebDocuments		155
		7.1.1	The Technology behind WebDocuments	156
		7.1.2	Configuration of WebDocuments	157
		7.1.3	An Example of Working in WebDocuments	160
	7.2	SAP Easy DMS		164
		7.2.1	SAP Easy DMS Installation	166
		7.2.2	SAP Easy DMS Configuration	166
		7.2.3	SAP Easy DMS and Microsoft Windows Explorer	166
		7.2.4	Controlling SAP Easy DMS via Registry Settings	167
		7.2.5	Additional Features When Working with Files in SAP Easy DMS	167
		7.2.6	Additional Features When Working with Folders in SAP Easy DMS	170
		7.2.7	Searching	171
		7.2.8	Editing Offline	172
		7.2.9	Adjusting the Layout	173
		7.2.10	Using Filters	174
		7.2.11	Effort for Implementing SAP Easy DMS	175
	7.3	SAP DMS Portal iView		175
	7.4	Summary		176

8 SAP PLM 7.02 DMS Web UI 177

- 8.1 Introducing the New Web UI for SAP DMS 177
- 8.2 Working with the SAP PLM 7.02 DMS Web UI 178
  - 8.2.1 Logging Into SAP PLM 7.02 DMS via SAP NetWeaver Business Client 178
  - 8.2.2 Create Document 179
  - 8.2.3 Populate General Data 180
- 8.3 Additional Features of the SAP PLM 7.02 Web UI 188
  - 8.3.1 My Objects 188
  - 8.3.2 Simple Search 189
  - 8.3.3 Advanced Search 191
  - 8.3.4 Side Panel 192
  - 8.3.5 "You Can Also" Functionality 192
  - 8.3.6 Object Navigator 193
  - 8.3.7 Personal Object Work List 194
  - 8.3.8 Document Browser 195
  - 8.3.9 Extended Document Browser 195
  - 8.3.10 SAP PLM Web UI Inbox 197
- 8.4 SAP PLM 7.02 DMS Web UI Additional Configuration Items 197
  - 8.4.1 SAP IMG Configuration Items 198
- 8.5 Summary 207

9 Integrating a CAD System to SAP DMS 209

- 9.1 Available SAP CAD Integration Interfaces 209
- 9.2 Capabilities and Benefits of CAD Interfaces 210
  - 9.2.1 Capabilities 210
  - 9.2.2 Benefits 211
- 9.3 SAP CAD Desktop 211
- 9.4 Example CAD Integration Scenario 213
- 9.5 CAD Data Migration 214
- 9.6 SAP Visual Enterprise Tools and CAD Data 214
- 9.7 Summary 215

10 Simple Document Approval Process using SAP Workflow ... 217

- 10.1 The Workflow Scenario ... 217
- 10.2 Required SAP DMS and Workflow Configuration ... 218
- 10.3 Creating the Workflow Definition ... 218
  - 10.3.1 Execute Transaction PFTC (Task: Maintain) ... 218
  - 10.3.2 Enter Information on the Basic Data Tab of the Workflow Definition ... 219
  - 10.3.3 Create New Container Element ... 220
  - 10.3.4 Save the Workflow Definition ... 222
  - 10.3.5 Add Triggering Event ... 223
  - 10.3.6 Start the Workflow Builder ... 223
  - 10.3.7 Set the Additional Start Conditions ... 224
  - 10.3.8 Add Tasks to the Workflow ... 225
  - 10.3.9 Activate the Workflow ... 231
- 10.4 Execute and Test the Workflow ... 231
- 10.5 Summary ... 233

11 SAP DMS BAdIs and User Exits ... 235

- 11.1 About SAP BAdIs and User Exits ... 235
- 11.2 BAdIs Relevant to SAP DMS ... 237
  - 11.2.1 BAdI DOCUMENT_MAIN01: General Document Processing ... 240
  - 11.2.2 BAdI DOCUMENT_THUMBNAIL: Enhancement for Thumbnails ... 241
  - 11.2.3 BAdI DOCUMENT_AUTH01: Checking Authorization from the DMS ... 242
  - 11.2.4 BAdI DOCUMENT_FILES01: Processing of Original Application Files ... 243
  - 11.2.5 BAdI DOCUMENT_STORAGE01: Transport of Original Application Files ... 244
  - 11.2.6 BAdI DOCUMENT_STATUS01: Status Checks ... 245
  - 11.2.7 BAdI DOCUMENT_MAIN02: Document Exits and Menu Enhancements ... 246
  - 11.2.8 BAdI DOCUMENT_NUMBER01: Checking the Attributes of the Document Key ... 247

		11.2.9	BAdI: DOCUMENT_PROC01: Filter for SAP DMS Processes	247
		11.2.10	BAdI DOCUMENT_WEB01: Enhancements for the DMS@Web Scenarios	248
		11.2.11	BAdI DOCUMENT_OFFINTEGR01: Enhancements for Microsoft Office Integration	249
		11.2.12	BAdI DOCUMENT_ECL01: Displaying Original Application Files with the Viewer	249
		11.2.13	BAdI CONVERTER_MAIN01: Exits during Conversion	250
	11.3	User Exits Available in SAP DMS		251
	11.4	Enhancement of SAP DMS in PLM 7.01		252
	11.5	Summary		252

12 Conclusion ... 253

	12.1	SAP DMS: Now You Know It		253
		12.1.1	Introduction	253
		12.1.2	Questions to Answer before Starting Your SAP DMS Project	254
		12.1.3	SAP DMS Step-by-Step Instructions	254
		12.1.4	Configuring SAP DMS	254
		12.1.5	Infrastructure Requirements	255
		12.1.6	SAP DMS Security	255
		12.1.7	Frontends to SAP DMS	255
		12.1.8	SAP PLM 7.02 DMS WebUI	256
		12.1.9	Integrating a CAD System to SAP DMS	256
		12.1.10	Simple Document Approval Process using SAP Workflow	256
		12.1.11	SAP DMS BAdIs and User Exits	257
	12.2	The Future of SAP DMS		257
	12.3	Summary		257

Appendices			**259**
A	Glossary		261
B	Review of Menu Items		265
	B.1	Menu Option Document	265
	B.2	Menu Option Edit	266
	B.3	Menu Option Goto	266
	B.4	Menu Option Extras	266
	B.5	Menu Option Environment	267
	B.6	Menu Option Originals	268
	B.7	Additional Resources	269
C	The Author		271

Index ... 273

This introduction to SAP Document Management System includes its benefits and project requirements.

1 Introduction

In this chapter, you'll learn what SAP Document Management System (DMS) is and how you can benefit from its implementation. You'll also learn about project complexity and the types of resources you should plan to have on your project.

This chapter also reviews how this book should be used and its structure to progress from simple to complex topics. Finally, in this chapter, you'll learn about the availability of SAP DMS in different releases of SAP software.

1.1 What Is SAP DMS?

SAP DMS is an enterprise document management system that you can use to manage documents for your business. Surprisingly, many companies aren't aware this. This functionality isn't part of an add-on or an additional piece of software you must purchase from SAP. Rather, it's part of your base SAP ERP system. With a little basic knowledge of SAP DMS and its configuration, you can begin to take advantage of SAP DMS functionality in your system, such as the following:

- Secure storage for documents
- Check-in/check-out functionality
- Ability to classify documents for searching
- Linking of documents to other objects for visibility across the system
- Integration of Microsoft® Office applications for updating documents
- Elaborate security profiles to protect access to documents

- Controlling of documents through the change management process
- Use of versions and revisions
- Full-text search across stored documents
- Automatic conversion of documents to neutral format for viewing and long-term storage
- Integration of your CAD system into SAP DMS for management of drawings and models

This is a brief list of the functionalities offered by SAP DMS. In this book, you'll learn about all of these and much more.

1.2 Benefits of SAP DMS

Using SAP DMS, and a document management system in general, provides many benefits. Companies and individuals generate large numbers of documents each day. These documents are the lifeblood of most companies, and without them, companies can't exist.

The documents may be stored on a person's laptop, kept on a shared drive, or hidden in someone's desktop drawer. People need access to these documents to make business decisions. Access to documents needs to be fast; people can't spend hours or days searching for the right information. This is where SAP DMS comes into play. Using SAP DMS, you can take all of the key business documents your company is generating and store them in one place that everyone can use as the source of information. This is a major business benefit.

When implementing SAP DMS, you can expect to experience the following benefits for your business.

- Secure storage of documents
- Easy retrieval of documents
- Excellent search capabilities to cut down on time searching for documents
- Controlled environment for updates to documents
- Complex security rules to control access

- Increased visibility of key documents
- One source and one set of rules for managing documents
- Reduced time and effort spent on document management
- Ability to maintain document history to meet legal requirements

These are just a few of the possible business benefits of SAP DMS, and depending on your environment, you may have a completely different set of business challenges to solve and benefits to achieve. SAP DMS offers many benefits to all companies that own SAP software and generate documents. Implementing and using SAP DMS is therefore something every company should consider.

1.3 SAP DMS Project Complexity

In general, SAP DMS projects aren't the most complex projects in the SAP world. They aren't as complex as setting up finance or manufacturing, for example. In fact, they are typically light in terms of configuration and transactions. The complexity of an SAP DMS project is driven by the number of different types of documents you want to manage and by the rules for each document. In a complex project, for example, you might want to manage all documents generated by your engineering, finance, and purchasing departments. Let's imagine this includes more than 300 unique types of documents. For each unique document, you have to think about rules, such as the following: How do I want to search for the document? What is its lifecycle? What are the security rules? These are just a few of the rules that need to be defined.

In a simpler project, you might only want to manage documents coming from a customer and have them attached to the appropriate customer record in the SAP system. This is a simple and straightforward project because you're working on developing rules for only one type of document.

As mentioned previously, project complexity increases with the number of different types of documents to be managed.

1.4 Resources Required for a Project

An SAP DMS implementation project requires a varied set of resources, including the following:

- **Business users**
  Business personnel must know about the rules for the documents that are being stored, such as who needs to approve a document before it becomes official. Business users will work with the SAP application consultant to map out a process for the documents being stored.

- **SAP application consultant**
  The SAP application consultant works with business users to define a process for each document being stored. After this process is defined, SAP application consultants map it to the SAP system and complete the SAP configuration.

- **SAP Basis/IT infrastructure resources**
  The SAP Basis/IT infrastructure resources set up the infrastructure components required to support SAP DMS. This includes items such as content servers, cache servers, TREX, and conversion servers. Setting up the infrastructure components is usually one of the first activities accomplished in a project.

You may have one or several of each of these resource types, depending again on the number of documents you plan to store in the system.

1.5 How to Use This Book

As mentioned earlier, this book proceeds from simple to complex topics. In Chapter 2, you'll start by answering some basic business questions, such as what types of documents you want to manage, and what attributes are associated with these documents. Answering these questions is important because it sets you up to start thinking about how your SAP DMS implementation will function. Chapter 3 reviews how to execute basic SAP DMS transactions, and step-by-step instructions are provided. Next, in Chapter 4, you'll tackle how to configure the system. This means that you'll learn how to set up items such as document types, additional attributes, and status networks. After you've completed the configuration, you can begin to use the system to store your documents.

The chapters that follow take you through more advanced topics such as defining and setting up security, infrastructure requirements, and the use of BAdIs or user exits to enhance the basic functionality provided by SAP.

You will note that the book includes marginal notes where relevant. An example of a marginal note is located to the right in the margin. These notes will help you quickly identify additional topics within a section.

This is a marginal note.

The overall goal of the book is to prepare you for the implementation and use of SAP DMS in your environment. After reading this book and learning the material, you'll not only have a thorough understanding of what SAP DMS is, but you'll also be able to configure and use it effectively.

If you're a beginner with SAP DMS, it's best to proceed through the chapters in sequence. As mentioned previously, you'll start with the simple and move to the complex, and each chapter will build on the knowledge you gained in the one before it. Advanced chapters assume that you've understood the content in the previous chapters. More advanced readers can start with the chapters they are interested in learning about. As an example, if you understand the SAP DMS transactions and configuration activities but need information on how to set up SAP DMS security, you can go directly to the chapter that covers security.

1.6 A Note on the Availability of SAP DMS

SAP DMS is available in SAP R/3 3.1 and up. This book is written based on the SAP DMS functionality available in SAP ECC 6.0, EhP 6. This is a modern release; however, you'll find most of the SAP DMS functionality described in this book available in much earlier releases of SAP R/3, such as 4.6 and 4.7. Therefore, you don't need to upgrade your system to the latest SAP release to take advantage of SAP DMS functionality. Most likely, you can start working immediately using the release you have today. If you want to take advantage of SAP Product Lifecycle Management (SAP PLM) 7.02 DMS functions, however, you'll need to have an SAP ECC 6.0 system at EhP 6. For SAP PLM 7.01, you'll need an SAP ECC 6.0 system at EhP 5. Please refer to Chapter 8 for a full discussion of SAP PLM 7.01 and 7.02. In that chapter, we'll discuss the benefits of the new Web UI, including the addition of status management in SAP PLM 7.02.

1.7 Summary

In this chapter, we've provided a brief introduction to SAP DMS. Through SAP DMS, SAP provides you with an enterprise document management system you can use without purchasing additional software. Some of the benefits of implementing SAP DMS include easy retrieval, secure storage, and the ability to apply complex security rules for document access.

You were then given an idea of how to judge project complexity based on the number of different documents you plan to manage. You also learned about the three different types of resources required for an SAP DMS project: business users, SAP application consultants, and SAP Basis/IT infrastructure resources. Finally, you learned how to use this book, and about the general availability of SAP DMS across SAP software releases.

In Chapter 2, we'll identify questions you need to answer before starting your SAP DMS project.

This chapter reviews information you need to address before starting your SAP DMS project. This is the foundation to making sure your project will be successful.

2   Questions to Answer before Starting Your SAP DMS Project

Before starting your SAP DMS project, there are a number of questions you need to answer and considerations that you should take into account. At this point in the process, your focus should be more on defining your requirements and goals and less on what SAP DMS can do. After you prepare a solid foundation and plan, the information can be used effectively when you begin configuring and using SAP DMS.

Defining your requirements and goals is critical to project success. It's much easier to reach a goal efficiently with planning and insight. This chapter discusses the basic considerations you need to address before starting your SAP DMS project.

2.1   Defining Which Documents to Manage with SAP DMS

The first step in your SAP DMS project is defining the documents you want to manage. On a daily basis, a business can generate thousands of documents, which make up the intellectual capital and value of that business. Some generated documents are trivial, whereas others are critical to the production and sale of products. Critical documents include CAD drawings, test reports, product specifications, product literature, and financial documents. Without these critical documents, a company can't create, purchase, or sell goods. These are the types of documents that should be managed within SAP DMS.

If a company is using SAP software, business processes such as manufacturing, sales, purchasing, engineering, and finance are likely being executed and managed within the SAP system. When selecting which documents to manage within SAP DMS, you should select documents that support such business processes. Key documents are then gathered into one location where the business process is being executed. This makes the data more widely available and less difficult to find, and allows updates to be managed in a controlled manner.

> **Example**
> You want to manage all documents associated with the engineering change process you execute within the SAP system. Multiple documents are generated and controlled through this process, and these documents should be stored within SAP DMS.

2.2 How Documents Fit Into the Overall Business Process

The next important step is defining how the documents you want to manage fit into the overall business process with which they are associated. Are documents created or required at certain steps in the process? With which business objects are documents associated? Map out your business in a process flow. For each step in the flow, you can identify which documents are required. You should look at what is significant about each document and what it feeds downstream or what it triggers.

For example, it's a best practice that each company has a process for the development and introduction of new products. During this process, certain documents are required to move to the next phase or maturity level of the product design. If you're in the "prototype" phase of your product design, you'll need drawings released at a certain status, signifying that they can be used to build prototypes but not production parts. Along with the drawings, you may need documents such as specifications and finite elements analysis reports.

> **Example**
>
> Imagine that you work for a company that produces bicycles. Before a bicycle can be shipped from the factory, a document describing how the bicycle should be assembled by the consumer must be stored in the system, printed, and included as part of the overall package.
>
> The assembly instructions are related to the finished good item material master for the bicycle in the SAP system and may be included as an item in the bill of materials (BOM). You might also have a business process or system check in place to make sure that the assembly instructions are stored in the SAP system before manufacturing and shipping of the bicycle can happen.

2.3 How to Search for Stored Documents

With SAP DMS, you aren't just storing files or attachments. Along with the files, you're also storing attributes. Examples of standard attributes stored with each file include the following:

- Description
- Owner
- Responsible lab office

Along with standard attributes, you can store additional attributes, which can be used to search for stored documents.

For example, if you're storing CAD drawings you might want to know in which CAD application and release of the application the drawings were created. You might also want to know the size of the drawing and which customers are using it. These are a few examples of additional attributes you might want to maintain.

This is an important topic, and you should make the necessary effort to define and add document attributes that are required to fulfill your search requirements. This will prevent you from creating an unstructured and unsearchable system.

> **Example**
>
> You plan on storing the resumes of all of your employees. When new positions or opportunities become available, you want to be able to search across the resumes to find qualified internal candidates, using the following attributes:
> - Employee location
> - Salary category (hourly, salaried)
> - Willing to relocate
> - Skill set
> - Languages spoken
> - Education level
>
> Searching on these attributes will return a list of resumes that match the selection criteria.

2.4 Define the Lifecycle of Documents

Each document can have a lifecycle of its own. Think of a lifecycle as the time from which the document was created to when it becomes obsolete. Steps in between can include times when the document is in one of the following states:

- In work
- Pending approval
- Approved
- Released

At each step of the lifecycle, the SAP system can be configured to act in a certain way or perform certain actions, such as sending notifications when a document reaches the released state.

> **Example**
>
> When a document is in the released state, you can specify that no further updates can be made to the document without creating a new version. The released version remains as history in the system. Imagine that the released version relates to a certain design or release level of a product you are building. Because it remains as history in the system, you can always track back to the documentation that was used to build the product at that specific design or release level.

2.5 The Change Control Process

Another item you need to address and plan for before implementing SAP DMS is the change control process. That is, for documents being stored, you need to determine whether updates are controlled through a change control process. A change control process can involve controlling changes to a document through the SAP Engineering Change Management in the SAP system. This is a formal and rigorous process that can include capturing a reason for changes, elements of workflow, and required digital signatures for release. A formal change control process provides you with a complete history of when and why a document was updated, which is important for documents that are critical to business operation.

> **Example**
> Let's take the case of CAD drawings again. Manufacturing depends on these drawings to build the product in a correct manner. If there is no change process in place for these drawings, someone could update them at will and never communicate the changes. As a result, the engineering group might have one idea of how the product looks, and manufacturing might have another, different idea. A business can't operate in such a manner for any amount of time.

2.6 A Formal Approval Process

Before a document can become an official released version, it may have to go through a formal approval process. Typically, documents that are critical to the design and manufacturing of a product, such as CAD drawings, specifications, and design failure mode effects analysis, go through a formal approval process. This process can be facilitated through a workflow process and might require a digital signature. With a digital signature, the user is required to input a user name and password or other type of security information to validate that the user is signing off on or approving the document. The result of the formal approval is a released version of the document with a record of who approved it. Any further changes to the document can be made only by creating a new version.

Workflow process

> **Example**
> When a document reaches the Review status, a workflow process is started that sends a workflow notification to a reviewer. The reviewer reviews the document and decides if it should be released or sent back for rework. If the person decides that the document needs rework, he puts the document back into a status of "In Work" and provides the appropriate commentary back to the person who requested the review. If approved, the document is set to a status of "Released" and is locked to prevent further change. For additional changes to the document, a new version must be created. The released version remains in the system as history.

2.7 Identify Business Roles and Mapping

You need to make an effort to identify the different business roles that will be interacting with SAP DMS. This role mapping allows connections to process activities and which roles are connected to what people (and jobs) in the "to-be" process. Map the following to each identified role:

- Activities they will carry out
- Number of individuals in each role
- Where the individuals reside (if you have several business locations)
- Training they will require

Identifying the roles allows you to build a complete use case for SAP DMS that goes beyond just looking at a simple set of transaction codes.

2.8 Security Requirements

Next, you need to address security requirements for each document. Consider the following questions:

- What roles in the business are allowed to change each document?
- Does the document status need to be taken into consideration?
- When a document is in In Work status, should a select group be able to view it?

▸ When the document is released, should it be opened for everyone to view?

For example, all CAD drawings are viewable by everyone after they are released for production. A "released for production" design means that the manufacturing group is building a production product and that product is being sold to the consumer. Therefore, the design can be deconstructed and analyzed. Before a design is released for production, while in a "prototype" or "early development" stage, only the project team that is working on the design has access to view or change the drawings. This reduces the possibility of design secrets getting out before the product is released.

The SAP system provides a complex set of conditions you can use to control access to documents. Several conditions can be combined, including document type, status, and authorization group assigned to the document.

> **Tip**
> You can set up SAP DMS so that, for example, only a person in the role of Document Control under project F1100 can view documents that are in a status of "Pending Review." After this is done, no other roles will have access.

2.9 Defining Which Type of Application Files to Store

Defining the type of application files to be stored within SAP DMS is important. The term *application file* is defined as the output file of a specific application. Sample applications include Microsoft Word, Excel, and PowerPoint. Each application can be configured in the SAP system to behave in a certain manner when an associated file is launched for display or change.

To define the appropriate application file types, take a look around your business and see what applications are being used. Most likely, it's a basic set of applications. The SAP system doesn't restrict the type of application files that can be stored. Therefore, you can store the output of just about any application in SAP DMS.

2.10 Document Numbering

Document numbering needs to be covered during every SAP DMS project. Companies have adopted various number schemes for differing reasons. In some cases, companies are using intelligent number schemes, where specific elements of the document number have specific meanings, are human readable, and may have developed out of a lack of having a computer-based system for managing documents. Some companies will have adapted to the idea that numbers have no meaning and are just numbers used to identify the document. In relation to SAP DMS, you need to think about how document numbers will be utilized. Every document stored in SAP DMS will be assigned a number as a system requirement. SAP DMS supports assigning internally generated sequential numbers to documents. SAP DMS also supports assigning an external number, which means that it can support intelligent document numbers if required. An external number may be alphanumeric, while internal numbers are purely numeric.

> **Best Practice**
> When doing implementations, we recommend using an internally generated number for documents as a best practice. Following this practice matches best with how the SAP system functions and limits user input.

2.11 Change History Requirements

SAP DMS keeps excellent track of all changes being made to documents stored within the system, including but not limited to, updates to attributes, when object links change, description changes, status changes, and each time a file check-in/check-out occurs. You will want to define your very specific change history requirements to make sure SAP is capturing everything required for your specific use case. As an example, you might consider having a requirement to record each time someone views a document. Some industries have additional audit requirements, in which the SAP change records may need to be extended. The process of extending the change records can be accomplished via enhancements using standard delivered SAP Business Add-Ins (BAdIs).

> **Example**
> Company A makes military goods. Documents related to its product designs are stored in SAP DMS. Due to legal requirements, any time a user changes a document, who changed the document and when must be recorded. The change record in SAP DMS captures this information as part of the standard change record.

2.12 Versions and Revisions

A *version* in SAP DMS is defined as a separate instance of a document information record that has its own status, such as In Work or Released. It is a snapshot in time. A *revision* level is assigned to a document version and is associated with a release state. It's usually used as a representation of a major change. For each document, you can store multiple versions. With each version, you can assign a revision identifier.

It's important to clarify what these terms mean to your business because they can become confusing. When you start to work with the system and start to speak of versions and revisions, each person may have a different picture in mind because, at times, the terms are interchangeable.

For example, you might create a document and store it in SAP DMS. On storing, an initial version of 00 is assigned to the document. Let's say you then decide that you want to save your work as a snapshot at version 00. To do so, you can create a new version of the document, to which version 01 is assigned. When your work on version 01 of the document is complete, you want to release this as an official revision of the document. You can release the document through a change control process that associates revision A to version 01. The "revision" indicator identifies to your business users that the document is an officially released document. Further changes will be made to version 02 of the document, and it may take many additional versions until a revision B is created.

Version and revision example

2.13 Management of Content Versions

Within a specific version of a stored document, SAP DMS has the capability to store content versions of the files stored. A content version for a file is created each time the user checks in a file after a check-out. This allows for a complete history of updates made to the file. The system enables you to activate an earlier version of a file if required. This is a nice function if a later version has become corrupted or you've decided to go back to an earlier version. This feature allows you to also meet cases where by law or for liability, you're required to manage a complete history of file updates.

2.14 Searching and Maintenance in Multiple Languages

You should also consider whether you'll need to maintain certain attributes, such as "description," in multiple languages. This requirement is not uncommon in large companies that have locations and employees across the globe with business transactions performed in multiple languages. For such situations, the SAP system provides you with the capability to maintain entry, display, and searching of attributes in multiple languages. It is a good idea to plan for this up front because you'll need to take this into consideration when configuring the SAP system.

2.15 Full-Text Search Requirements

TREX

Beyond basic searching on attributes (e.g., description, status, owner), SAP DMS offers you the capability to perform full-text searches on stored documents. As part of its overall capabilities, SAP NetWeaver Search and Classification (colloquially known as TREX) allows you to create a full-text searchable index of all documents stored within SAP DMS. Full-text searching capability is popular among users because it allows them to easily search across all stored documents with keywords. An additional advantage with full-text search is that TREX searching is much faster than a database search.

> **Example**
>
> Due to a product change, you need to find all documents that reference part # "P100". As part of the basic SAP DMS search transaction, you can enter a search term of "P100", and all indexed documents with "P100" referenced will be returned.

2.16 Stored Document Volume and Size

Having an idea of the volume of documents to be stored is helpful because the infrastructure, and specifically the content server, will need to be sized differently to support, for example, 10 thousand versus 10 million documents.

Also, understanding the average size of files being stored will help with network sizing. Document consumers will likely exist in a number of different geographic locations. Depending on where content servers are located, users viewing or changing documents stored in SAP DMS will be accessing files across a wide area network (WAN), which will impact the network's usage and sizing.

> **Example**
>
> At your company, the creators of CAD data are located in the Detroit office, where the content server is also located. The CAD data can be between 10MB and 35MB per file.
>
> Individuals using the CAD data are located across the globe, in Europe and Asia. Each time an individual from Europe or Asia views the CAD data, it's accessed across the WAN and downloaded to the local PC. Because the files are very large, this can have a major impact on WAN utilization and on the time the user spends waiting for the document.
>
> To address this, you can install a cache server at the different remote locations. Data is then cached at the remote site the first time it is viewed. Additional requests by individuals at the remote location will first go to the cache server to see if documents can be accessed there; only if this is not possible, will the requests go to the remote content server. If files can be pulled from the cache server, response times for delivering the files to users will be quicker, thereby decreasing the impact on the WAN's performance.

2.17 Locations for Document Creators versus Consumers

It's also best to identify the different geographic locations of creators and consumers of documents. A *creator* is someone who generates and stores documents in the system. A *consumer* is someone who searches for documents and displays them. If there are a large number of document creators at a specific location, such as at an engineering center, the site may require the installation of a local content server. At locations with a high number of document consumers, such as manufacturing plants, it might be beneficial to install a cache server. Following these two concepts will help decrease the impact on the performance of your WAN.

2.18 Document Retention Requirements

Document retention requirements define how long a document should be stored or be available based on business and legal requirements. Therefore, you need to review what your retention requirements are per document.

For example, in the construction industry, it's considered a best practice to retain all construction drawings and specifications for an indefinite period. Also, studies and reports that relate to a building's design must be maintained indefinitely.

Retention periods It's also best to address how a document should be handled after the retention period has passed. That is, you need to decide whether it should be archived or deleted. Considering document retention requirements is important mainly because the system must support the legal requirements of the business. If a lawsuit is brought forward against your company, you must be able to produce documents that support your case. In the case of product liability lawsuits, not being able to produce proper documentation can lead to catastrophic results.

> **Example**
>
> Your company has decided to keep all CAD data related to a product's design for a total of 15 years after the start of the product's production. When this period has been passed, all CAD data will be deleted from the system if the product is no longer being manufactured. To accomplish this, a process runs daily in the SAP system to see if any documents have passed the retention period. If so, they are marked for deletion. Then, using a different process, documents are permanently deleted from the system.

2.19 Conversion to Neutral Format for Long-Term Retention

For long-term retention, documents can be converted from their original application file format to a neutral file format such as TIF or PDF. If document retention requirements state that a document should be kept for the next 20 years, it's almost certain that the application the file was originally created in will no longer function at that point in the future. "Neutral" file formats such as TIF and PDF help solve this problem.

> **Example**
>
> On the release of product and packaging specifications stored in SAP DMS, all associated files are converted from the original Word format to the PDF format. This conversion is carried out automatically by the SAP system when the status of "Released" is reached. The trigger for the conversion is controlled through the SAP Implementation Guide (IMG) configuration and carried out on a conversion server, which is a component of the SAP Knowledge Provider.

2.20 Interface with External Systems

If you'll need to interface to any external systems to pull documents from or push documents to, SAP has a robust interfacing-facing technology, including SAP NetWeaver Process Integration (SAP NetWeaver PI), to support both options. This is an important consideration as you plan the correct infrastructure components to support such an interface.

> **Example**
> As part of controlled change process, specific documents are released in System A. These documents also need to be stored in SAP DMS for consumption by users in SAP. During the release process in System A, a message is sent from System A to SAP NetWeaver PI where the message is transformed and forwarded to the related SAP system. When the message is received in SAP, a document record is created in SAP DMS with the original file attached.

2.21 Data Migration Requirements

As part of your project, you'll likely have documents that need to be migrated from an external location into SAP DMS. Consider the following questions when planning your data migration:

- Where is the current location of the documents to be migrated?
- How many documents will be migrated?
- What is the average size of each file to be migrated?
- Which attributes will be migrated with each file?
- Are there relationships between files that need to be built as part of the migration?
- Will only the current version of a document be migrated or will all historical versions be migrated? (Try to spend time determining the value of historical versions before migrating everything.)
- If documents are stored in a legacy system, how will documents and attribute data be extracted?
- What are the validation procedures to confirm that documents are coming into SAP DMS correctly?

Planning your data migration is a crucial step to having a successful SAP DMS project. Answering the preceding questions can help you get a good grasp of the complexity of the migration and plan accordingly.

2.22 Training

You must consider how training will be carried out and how you might tailor it to different groups of users. For example, you may have some users who just need to log in to the system and display documents. Their training will be relatively simple in comparison to an administrator type role. The administrator might be responsible for creating, changing, and deleting documents, which requires additional training time.

For training methodology, consider what will be handled in classroom training, online training, or possibly prerecorded training. Classroom training is the most likely delivery method as the complexity of the activities to perform increases.

> **Tip**
> In an earlier section of this chapter, we asked that you start to think about high-level roles. You can use these roles as a starting point for mapping training requirements.

2.23 Organizational Change Impact

Now, take time to look at the organizational change management (OCM) aspects of implementing SAP DMS. When implementing SAP DMS, activities that individuals currently do will surely change, and new responsibilities and tasks will be created. The goal here is to document these activities and how they impact individuals. Some of the benefits of OCM include the following:

- Change is identified early in the process.
- Roles and responsibility changes are communicated earlier in the process. The surprise factor is removed because individuals know what to expect.
- Individuals have more time to prepare for change.
- Risks can be identified early, allowing for overall project risk to be reduced.

> **Example**
> Company A has a process where an individual receives released documents from the Engineering group via email and then logs into a system to store the released file. In the future, the Engineering group will directly log in to the SAP system and store the released files. In this case, the individual who was receiving the documents via email can now focus on more value-added activities.

2.24 Summary

In this chapter, we've reviewed important issues you need to address before an SAP DMS implementation. It's important that you define your goals and prepare for moving into the next steps of your SAP DMS project: using and configuring the system.

You should have answers to the following questions:

- What documents do you want to manage with SAP?
- How do documents fit in to the overall business process?
- How do you want to search for documents?
- What is the change control process?
- Is there a formal approval process?
- Which business roles are involved in the process?
- What are the security requirements?
- What type of application files will be stored?
- Do you have any special requirements around document numbering? Will you use internal or external numbering?
- Are there any special change history requirements?
- How are versions and revisions used in your business?
- Will you maintain content versions for stored files?
- Do you need to support searching and maintenance in multiple languages?
- Do you need to enable full-text searching capabilities?
- What is the volume and size of documents to be stored?

- Are there document retention requirements?
- Do documents need to be converted to a neutral format for long-term retention?
- Will you be interfacing with external systems?
- What are the data migration requirements?
- Who needs to be trained? What training methodology do you expect to use?
- How will implementing SAP DMS impact your organization?

The more clearly you can answer these questions, the more successful your project will be in the long run.

Next, in Chapter 3, you'll learn how to execute basic SAP DMS transactions and other functions.

This chapter presents instructions you need to execute SAP DMS and other related transactions.

3   SAP DMS Step-by-Step Instructions

In this chapter you'll learn how to execute SAP DMS and related transactions for creating, changing, displaying, and searching for document information records. You'll also learn about ancillary transactions such as the Product Structure Browser and Classification Search. It's important to have a good understanding of how the transactions covered in this chapter operate before proceeding with the configuration activity. Spending time executing these transactions will make learning and understanding the configuration process much easier.

3.1   SAP DMS Transactions

Table 3.1 lists the SAP DMS and related transactions that will be demonstrated in this chapter. You'll be given step-by-step instructions for executing each transaction. These are the main transactions you need to focus on learning for the proper configuration of SAP DMS.

SAP Transaction	Description
CV01N	Create Document
CV02N	Change Document
CV03N	Display Document
CV04N	Find Document
CC04	Product Structure Browser
CL30N	Find Document In Class

Table 3.1 SAP DMS and Related Transactions

3.2 Transaction CV01N: Creating a Document Information Record

The first thing you'll learn in this chapter is how to create a document information record. This is the beginning of creating an SAP DMS system; all other actions follow this action. By creating the record, you're initiating the record in the system, after which you can carry out the display and change actions, as well as many other actions.

3.2.1 Execute Transaction CV01N (Create Document)

On the initial screen, the first item you need to concern yourself with is selecting the document type. For this exercise, select DOCUMENT TYPE DRW (Eng./Des. Drawing), which is the standard document type delivered by SAP. The document type is a high-level classification of what type of document you'll be creating. It drives items such as status network, additional attributes, security, and other rules.

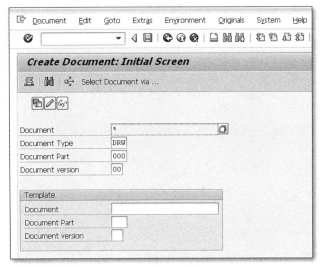

Figure 3.1 Transaction CV01N: Initial Screen

As shown in the screen in Figure 3.1, you can also enter a DOCUMENT NUMBER, DOCUMENT PART, and DOCUMENT VERSION. However, for this exercise, don't enter any values into these fields. The SAP system will automatically assign correct values based on how this document type is configured. This configuration will be explained in Chapter 4, which discusses how to configure SAP DMS.

When you've entered the DOCUMENT TYPE, press Enter to move to the next screen.

3.2.2 Fill Out Relevant Fields on the Document Data Tab

You must now fill out the following relevant fields on the DOCUMENT DATA tab of the document information record: DESCRIPTION, LAB OFFICE, CHANGE NUMBER, and AUTHORIZATION GROUP. A short description of each field on this tab is provided in Table 3.2.

Field	Description
DESCRIPTION	A short description of the document information record.
DOCUMENT STATUS	The current status of the document information record. When configuring a document type, an initial document status will usually be set. In this case, it's WR (WORK REQUEST).
CM RELEVANCE	Indicates if the object is controlled by Configuration Management.
USER	The person responsible for the document information record.
LAB OFFICE	The office or area of the business to which the document information record belongs.
CHANGE NUMBER	If the document is under change control, the number of the engineering change master is entered here.
AUTHORIZATION GROUP	The authorization group to which the document belongs. This field helps drive security.
SUPERIOR DOCUMENT	Helps determine a hierarchy. When assigned, you can display a simple document structure.
ORIGINALS	Area where you attach original files to the document information record.

Table 3.2 Description of Fields on the Document Data Tab

For this exercise, enter a DESCRIPTION and select a LAB OFFICE. Leave the other fields in the DOCUMENT DATA and SUPERIOR DOCUMENT areas as they are.

> **Adding Long Text**
>
> In this example, we're entering a short description for the document information record. You can enter a longer description by clicking on the CREATE LONG TEXT button next to the DESCRIPTION field. This lets you enter an unlimited amount of text that describes the document information record.

3.2.3 Add an Original File

Next, you need to add an original file to the document information record by clicking on either the CREATE ORIGINAL or OPEN ORIGINAL button on the ORIGINALS toolbar, as circled in Figure 3.2. Select a Word file, Excel file, or a text file from your desktop. After you select a file, you'll be asked to associate it to an application. If you selected a Word file, you'll want to associate it to the application type DOC or WRD. The application controls how the file is changed or displayed.

Figure 3.2 Adding Original Files

3.2.4 Check in an Original File

When you check in an original file to secure storage, it's stored back into the SAP database. As shown in Figure 3.3, you can click on the CHECK IN ORIG. button on the ORIGINALS toolbar. On the screen that appears, you need to select SAP DB as the storage data. Next, you need to select a storage category of SAP-SYSTEM. After making your selections, click on the green checkmark button to continue. You'll notice that the padlock symbol next to the original file is closed. This signifies that the file needs to be checked in. The actual movement of the file from your local system to the secure storage occurs when you save the document information record.

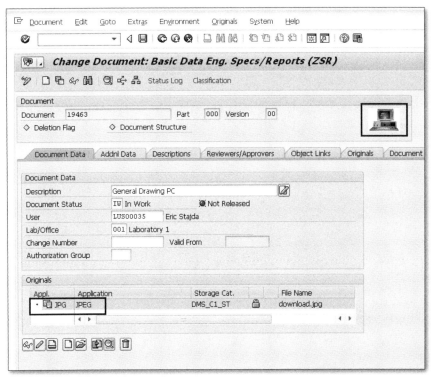

Figure 3.3 Document Data Tab Completed

3.2.5 Fill Out Attributes on the Addnl Data Tab

The ADDNL DATA tab contains attributes that help further define the document information record. The attributes appear on this tab because of the association of a default class to the document type during configuration. The class is defined using the SAP Classification System functionality and contains a definition for each attribute, including values and whether a specific attribute is required. Further information on setting up a class will be covered in Chapter 4.

The additional attributes are important because they are used to later search for the document information record. One of the key goals of having a document management system is the ability to search and locate documents quickly. A good deal of effort should be put into defining what additional attributes a user will be required to populate.

DRW attributes   For this exercise, the document type DRW has three additional attributes:

- FORM SIZE
- DATA CARRIER
- LINE NUMBER

Select a value from the value list associated with each attribute, "AO", "Paper", and "ACME", as shown in Figure 3.4.

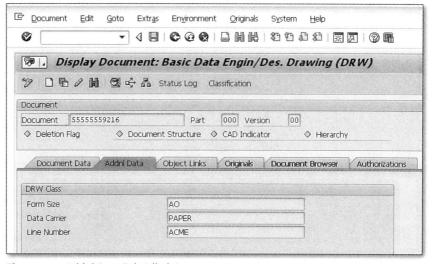

Figure 3.4 Addnl Data Tab Filled Out

3.2.6 Add a Language-Dependent Description

You can maintain multiple language-dependent descriptions for the document information record. If a user logs in to the SAP GUI with a different language, for example, French, the document information record description will appear in French, if it's maintained.

Language-dependent descriptions are maintained on the DESCRIPTIONS tab. For this exercise, select this tab, and enter the French description for the document information record by selecting the language FR and entering the description "Moi Document", as shown in Figure 3.5.

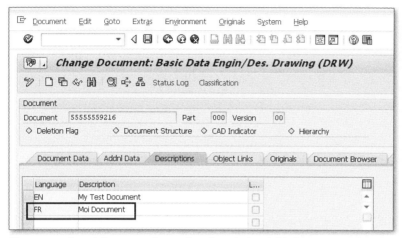

Figure 3.5 French Language-Dependent Description Added

3.2.7 Link the New Document to Another SAP Object

On the OBJECT LINKS tab, you can link a document information record to another object or record in the SAP system. Using object links is important because they allow you to connect a document information record to the supporting business object, which helps cut down on time spent searching for the relevant documentation.

> **Example**
>
> A customer has sent a set of documents that defines the requirements associated with bidding on projects and doing business together. These documents will be stored in SAP DMS. When they are stored, each document should be linked to the SAP customer record for that customer to make each document accessible from the SAP customer record. Therefore, employees looking at this record won't need to do a lot of searching to find documents that list requirements for bidding on projects and doing business with this customer.

Table 3.3 shows the object links that are possible with document type "DRW." Defining which objects a document record can be linked to will be covered in Chapter 4.

Object Links to Other SAP Objects		
Asset Master	General Notification	Production Versions
BOM Header	HR Master Link	Purchase Order Item
BOM Item	iPPE Variant	Purchase Req. Item
Change Number	Material Master	Quality Notification
Claim	Measuring Points	Reference Location
Class	Network Activity	Sales Document Item
cProjects Element	Object Link	SAP-EIS:Master Data
Customer	Plant Material	Vendor
Document Information Record	PPE Node	WBS Element
Equipment Master	Prod. Resource/Tool	
Functional Location	Production Order	

Table 3.3 Object Links Possible with Document Type "DRW"

Document information records

When you link a document information record to another SAP object, that document information record becomes visible in the corresponding transactions for that object. As illustrated in Figure 3.6, you link the document information record you're creating to a material master. To do this, on the OBJECT LINKS tab, select the MATERIAL MASTER tab. In the MATERIAL field, search for a material to link to. Any material master will do for this demonstration. In Figure 3.6, we've linked MATERIAL MASTER 50000402.

After the document information record is saved, you can open the linked material master through the Transaction MM02 (Change Material) and see the link between the document information record and the material master (see Figure 3.7).

3.2 Transaction CV01N: Creating a Document Information Record

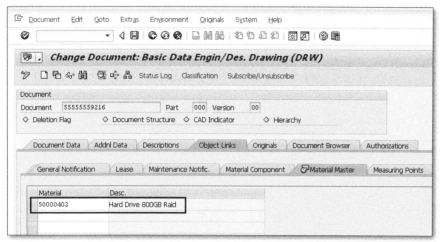

Figure 3.6 Document Information Record Linked to Material Master 3007-05

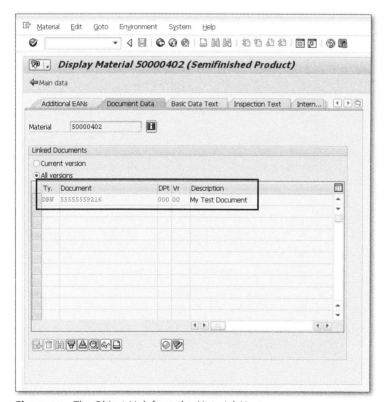

Figure 3.7 The Object Link from the Material Master

3.2.8 Save the Document Information Record

At this point, all of the required data has been entered for the document information record. You can now save the document information by clicking on the SAVE icon. Saving will initiate multiple actions:

1. Original files associated during the creation process will be moved from the local system into the SAP system.

2. A document number, part, and version will be assigned to the document information record.

On saving, as shown in Figure 3.8, you're returned to the initial creation screen showing the assigned document number, type, part, and version.

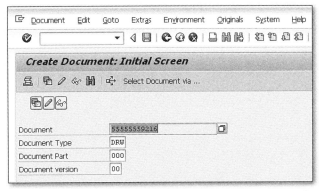

Figure 3.8 A Saved Document Information Record with Number, Type, Part, and Version Assigned

The creation process is now complete, and the document information record has been created in the SAP system. You can now move on to the change process.

3.3 Transaction CV02N: Changing a Document Information Record

Using Transaction CV02N (Change Document), you can now change the document information record you created earlier. Actions performed when changing a document information record can include the following:

Transaction CV02N: Changing a Document Information Record | 3.3

- Update basic or additional attributes
- Change the document status
- Add additional objects links
- Create a new version of the document information record
- Change an original file
- Add another original file

You'll learn how to perform all of these actions using the step-by-step instructions that follow.

3.3.1 Execute Transaction CV02N (Change Document)

On the initial screen of Transaction CV02N (Change Document), select the document you want to change. For this exercise, use the document information record you created previously, and enter the document number, type, part, and version. If you don't remember the document number, use the PROCESSED DOCUMENTS button, circled in the toolbar in Figure 3.9, to locate document information records that you've previously worked on.

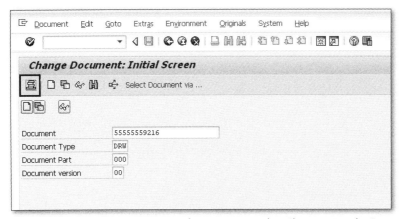

Figure 3.9 Selecting a Document Information Record to Change using the Processed Documents Button

After you specify the document number, type, part, and version, press `Enter` to open the document information record in change mode.

53

3.3.2 Update the Description Field and Lab Office

With the document information record in change mode, you can now make changes. For this exercise, update the DESCRIPTION field, and change the LAB/OFFICE to which the document information record belongs.

All changes made are recorded in the change history of the document information record. Displaying the change history will be covered later in Section 3.4.3, when we look at executing the transaction to display a document information record.

3.3.3 Change the Status of the Document Information Record

The current status of your document is WR or WORK REQUEST. Change the document status to IW or IN WORK. To do this, select the DOCUMENT STATUS field, and execute the search help (press [F4]). As shown in Figure 3.10, the list of statuses that can be set appears. From the list, select IW.

When setting this status, a screen will pop up asking you to make a status log entry. This short description to document the status change is recorded in the status log and is accessible by clicking on the STATUS LOG button.

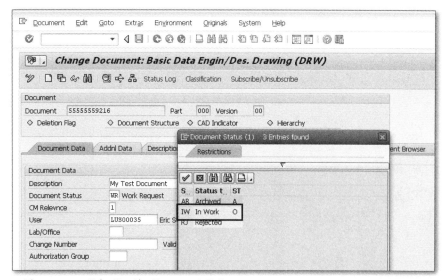

Figure 3.10 Selecting the Document Status

The document status represents where the document is at in its status network. A *status network* represents the lifecycle of the document information record. Each document type can have its own associated status network. Setting up a status network is covered in Chapter 4.

Document status

3.3.4 Add Object Links

When changing a document information record, you can add object links. For this exercise, link the document information record to a second material master. Or, if your system has customer information, link it to a customer. This demonstrates that it's possible to include additional object links, which is useful when the document information record is related to many different objects because it makes the related document information record visible on those objects.

3.3.5 Save the Document Information Record

All changes to be made to the document information record are now complete. Save the document information record. You'll be returned to the main screen of the change document transaction.

3.3.6 Create a New Version of the Document Information Record

To demonstrate another key capability, you'll now create a new version of the document information record: version "01". Version "00" will remain as it was last saved, and because it isn't released or locked, it's still possible to make changes to this version. The important concept to understand is that you now have two versions of the document information record. The document information records are still related, but each version can have its own original files, settings for attributes, and objects links.

To create a new version of the document information record, click on the NEW VERSION button circled in Figure 3.11. You'll be prompted to confirm that you want to create the new version based on version 00. Click on the CONTINUE button. You'll then be asked if you want to also copy the object links. This means that the new version will be linked to the same object as version 00. Confirm that you want to copy the objects links. You'll then be placed into change mode for version 01 of the document information record.

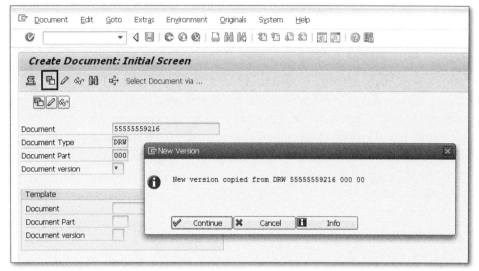

Figure 3.11 Creating a New Version of a Document Information Record

3.3.7 Check Out the Original File Associated with the New Version

Another important concept is changing an original file associated with a document information record. When you created the document information record, you associated an original Word, Excel, or other type of file. When the new version of the document information record was created, the original files were also copied to the new version. You'll now make changes to the original file associated with version 01 of the document information record. Afterward, you should take a look at the original file associated with version 00 of the document information record and note how they differ. The version 00 original files won't have the changes you made to the original files in version 01.

To change an original file, highlight the file in the ORIGINALS area of the DOCUMENT DATA tab, and click on the CHANGE ORIGINAL button, as circled in Figure 3.12.

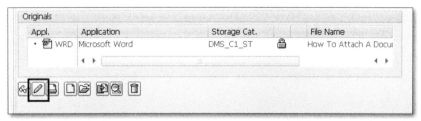

Figure 3.12 Selecting the Original File

You'll be prompted to provide a location on your local system where the original file will be checked out to, as shown in Figure 3.13. The default path is where the original file was checked in from, but you can specify a different path. After the check-out location has been selected, click on the CONTINUE button. The file is then opened in the appropriate application for updating. For this exercise, if your original file is a Word file, Word opens, and you can make your changes.

Check-out locations

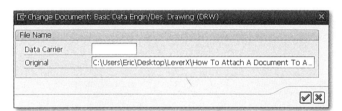

Figure 3.13 Selecting a Local Storage Location for the Check-Out File

For now, updates you're making are on a local copy of the original file. Other users can still access the original file to display it. When they do so, they access the latest copy that was stored in the SAP system. They can also see that the file is out for modification; the padlock icon is unlocked when a file is checked out, as shown in Figure 3.14.

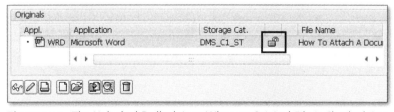

Figure 3.14 The Unlocked Padlock Icon When an Original File Is Checked Out

Make your updates to the original file and save. Close the application in which you were making changes.

3.3.8 Check in the Original File after Changes

After completing your changes, you need to check the original file back in. This moves the original file, with changes, from your local system back into the secure storage, making the updates you made accessible to other users.

When you checked out the original file for change, the system exited you from change mode on the document information record. To check in the original file, you need to open the document information record in change mode again. To check in the original file, highlight the original file, and click on the CHECK IN ORIG. button, as shown in Figure 3.15. After doing so, the padlock icon will once again lock, and the storage category will be populated. The actual movement of the file from your local system to the secure storage occurs when you save the document information record.

Figure 3.15 Check in the Original File after Making Changes

3.3.9 Add Another Original File to the New Version

You can have multiple original files associated with a document information record. To demonstrate this, open version 01 of the document information record you've been working on, and add another original file. Save the document information record.

The change process is now complete. Next, let's move on to the display process.

3.4 Transaction CV03N: Displaying a Document Information Record

Using Transaction CV03N (Display Document), you can display the document information record you created earlier. When displaying a document information record, you can review a variety of information. In this section, we'll go through step-by-step instructions for displaying key information. Keep in mind that it's also possible to review much of this information during the creation or change process.

Key items you might want to review when displaying a document information record include the following:

- An original file
- The status network
- The change history for the document information record
- The number of versions of the document information record

3.4.1 Display an Original File Associated with the Document Information Record

Using Transaction CV03N, open one of the document information records you created during the previous exercises. Double-click on one of the original files, or select the original file and then click on the DISPLAY ORIGINAL button. The original file opens in its corresponding application.

3.4.2 Display the Status Network

Each document type has a status network associated to it. As mentioned previously, the status network represents the lifecycle of the document information record. A simple example of a status network is that a document information record starts in the status of "In Work." At some point in time, a review needs to take place, and the document information record is set to a status of "In Review." After the review is held, and if everything is okay, the document information record status is set to "Released." This is the final state.

3 | SAP DMS Step-by-Step Instructions

To display the status network for a document information record, follow the menu path: EXTRAS • DISPLAY STATUS NETWORK. As shown in Figure 3.16, a popup screen appears with a graphical display of the status network.

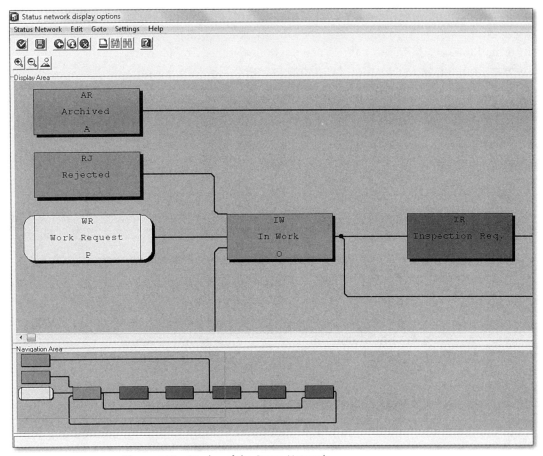

Figure 3.16 Display of the Status Network

Color display in the status network

You'll notice that statuses display in yellow, green, or red. Yellow represents the current status of the document information record. Green represents statuses that can be set. Red means that you can't set these statuses based on the current status of the document information record.

3.4.3 Review the Change History for the Document Information Record

It's important to be able to view the change history for a document information record. To have a controlled system, you need to know three basic elements: who has changed the data, when the data change occurred, and what specifically was changed. SAP software excels at capturing this type of information.

To display the change history for the document information record, follow the menu path: ENVIRONMENT • DISPLAY CHANGES. The result is shown in Figure 3.17.

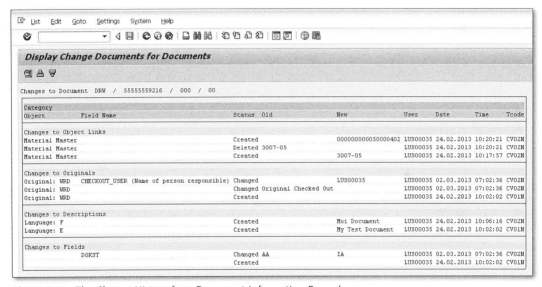

Figure 3.17 The Change History for a Document Information Record

The change history report is broken down into multiple sections, which include changes to objects, descriptions, and fields. As mentioned previously, with each change, you can find out who made the change, when the change was made, and what was changed.

Change history report

3.4.4 Check How Many Versions Are Available for a Document Information Record

When reviewing a document information record, it's important to be able check whether other versions of the document information record are available. For example, someone might have created a new version and might be in the process of making updates. To check whether other versions of the document information record are available, follow the menu path: EXTRAS • VERSIONS. As shown in Figure 3.18, you can see the other available versions of the document information record and the current status of those versions. You can open a version of the document information record by selecting and double-clicking it.

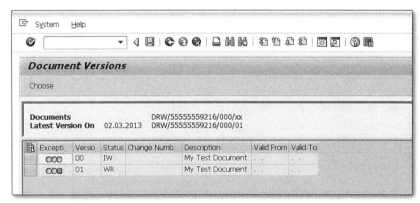

Figure 3.18 Displaying Available Document Versions

The display process is now complete. Next, let's move on to searching for the document information records you've created.

3.5 Transaction CV04N: Searching for a Document Information Record

Now that you've mastered the basic concepts of creating, changing, and displaying document information records, you'll next learn how to search for them. One of the key capabilities and benefits of implementing SAP DMS is the ability to search for what has been stored, and the search transaction allows you to find the proverbial needle in the haystack. Without search capabilities, you would only have a bunch of documents stored in a secure system, which would be no better than having the documents stored on a shared drive somewhere or placed in a folder on your desk.

Using Transaction CV04N (Find Document), you can search for documents using a variety of methods. This includes searching by the following:

- Basic document attributes
- Additional attributes or classifications
- Object links
- Texts or long text
- Full text

As shown in Figure 3.19, each method relates to a different tab in the FIND DOCUMENT transaction. You're not limited to searching by a single method or tab at a time; if you want, you can mix and match different methods. For example, you can find all document information records of type "DRW" that have the word "Pump" in their description. To execute this search, you need to enter search criteria on the DOCUMENT DATA (*) and TEXTS tabs.

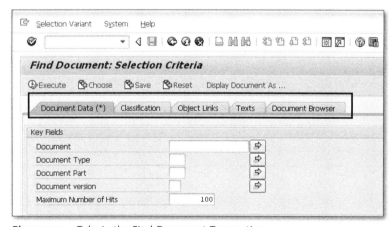

Figure 3.19 Tabs in the Find Document Transaction

3.5.1 Search for a Document Information Record by Document Type and User

In this first search example, you'll learn how to search by document type and user to get you acquainted with the use of the Find Document transaction.

The goal of this search is to find all document information records of type "DRW." This will locate all of the document information records you created earlier in this chapter.

As search criteria, enter "DRW" in the DOCUMENT TYPE field and your user name in the USER field as shown in Figure 3.20. Click on the EXECUTE button to start the search.

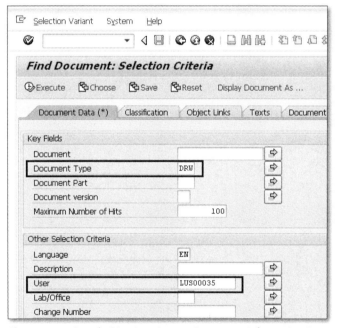

Figure 3.20 Search Criteria to Locate Document Information Records by Type and User

As shown in Figure 3.21, the document information records matching the search criteria are returned. You can double-click on a document information record in the list to open the record. From here, you can proceed with updating the document information record if required.

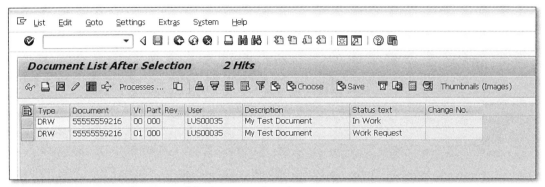

Figure 3.21 Search Results Returned for Document Search

3.5.2 Search for a Document Information Record by Document Type and Classification Attributes

Earlier in this chapter, you learned about the importance of the attributes maintained on the ADDNL DATA tab. Through the following example, we'll show you the benefit of these attributes. Defining and spending time figuring out which attributes should be associated with a document information record will pay off by decreasing the time users will spend searching.

For the example, you'll be using document type "DRW." This document type has an associated default class, which in turn has the following associated attributes or characteristics:

▶ FORM SIZE

▶ DATA CARRIER

▶ LINE NUMBER

For search criteria, enter the value "DRW" in the DOCUMENT TYPE field, and then select the CLASSIFICATION (*) tab. As shown in Figure 3.22, enter values for FORM SIZE and DATA CARRIER. Use the values you entered during the previous exercises. Click on the EXECUTE button to start the search. Document information records matching the search criteria will be returned.

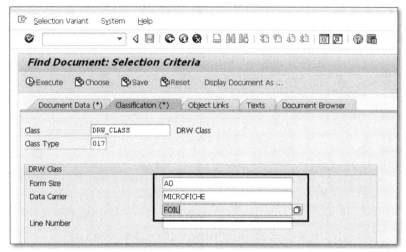

Figure 3.22 Searching by Classification of a Document Information Record

3.5.3 Search for a Document Information Record by Object Link

When you created document information records earlier in this chapter, you linked them to a material master. You can also find all document information records linked to a specific object. This is powerful because you can find all document information records related to a single object or set of objects in one search.

Material master object links

Select the OBJECT LINKS tab, and then select the MATERIAL MASTER tab. As shown in Figure 3.23, enter the material master number to which you linked your document information record in the earlier exercises. Click on the EXECUTE button to start the search. Document information records matching the search criteria will be returned.

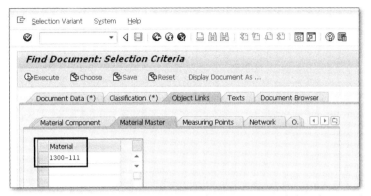

Figure 3.23 Searching for Document Information Records by Object Links

3.5.4 Search Long Text for a Document Information Record

You can search for document information records by long text. The long text is what is maintained beyond the short description. Instructions for maintaining long text were given earlier in Section 3.2.2.

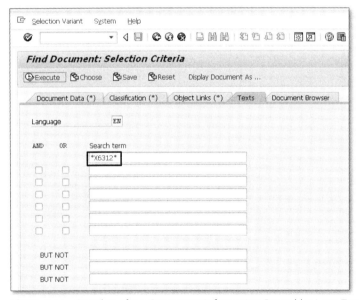

Figure 3.24 Searching for a Document Information Record by Long Text

To search for document information record by long text, select the TEXTS tab. As shown in Figure 3.24, under SEARCH TERM, enter a value to search for. You may use "*" as a wildcard character. You can also enter multiple values to search on, using the "and" and "or" operators.

After you've entered search criteria, click on the EXECUTE button to start the search. Document information records matching the search criteria will be returned.

3.5.5 Full-Text Search

You can also do a full-text search on the contents of original files that are stored in the system. The use of a full-text search requires a content server to be set up and the settings for indexing to be complete. These topics are discussed in Chapter 5, regarding the SAP DMS infrastructure.

To execute a full-text search, enter the term you want to search on in the SRCH TXT field. An example is shown in Figure 3.25. Click on the EXECUTE button to execute a full-text search through the original files that have been indexed by the indexing process. After searching through the index, the document information records that have original files associated with the search term will be returned in the search list.

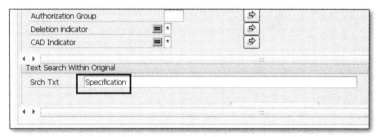

Figure 3.25 Searching for a Document Information Record using a Full-Text Search

3.6 Additional SAP DMS Functionalities

So far in this chapter, you've learned the basics of creating, changing, displaying, and searching for document information records. Let's move on to additional functionalities that can be used during the creation, change, or display processes. These functions cover a wide variety of activities you'll need to complete while working with document information records. They include everything from copying an existing document information record to setting a revision level.

3.6.1 Copy a Document Information Record

When creating a document information record using Transaction CV01N, you can copy from an existing document information record by filling in the information in the template area. This includes the document number, part, and version you want to copy from. All information from the template document information record will be copied to the new document information record.

3.6.2 Delete a Document Information Record

At times, you'll want to delete a document information record from the system. This is accomplished by setting the deletion indicator on the document information record you want to delete. To do so, open the document information record in change mode, and double-click on the selection box next to the DELETION FLAG field. As an alternative, choose DOCUMENT • CHANGE DELETION INDICATOR.

To actually delete a document information record, you need to execute Program MCDOKDEL using Transaction SE38.

3.6.3 Show the Sequence of Sources

To find out whether a document information record was copied from another document information record, follow the menu path: EXTRAS • SEQUENCES OF SOURCES. The report will also give you the sources for those document information records.

3.6.4 Creating and Displaying the Document Hierarchy

You can create a hierarchy of document information records by filling out the information in the SUPERIOR DOCUMENT area of the document information record. You identify a superior document by adding its document number, type, part, and version.

The hierarchy functionality is useful for relating document information records together. Through the hierarchy, you can identify one document record as part of a larger set of document information records.

To display the hierarchy, follow the menu path: EXTRAS • HIERARCHY. The report will show the complete hierarchy.

3.6.5 Display the Status Log

Information is recorded at each status change of the document information record. To review this information, follow the menu path: EXTRAS • STATUS LOG. Key information you'll find includes a record of when the status changed, who changed it, a short description, and also whether any digital signatures were made.

3.6.6 Set and Display Revision Levels

You can assign a revision level to a document information record. To do so, you must have a change number associated to the document information record, and one of the statuses in the status network must have the setting RELEASE FLAG checked. When this status is set, the system will prompt you concerning whether you want to assign a revision level to the document information record.

A revision level is often used as an indicator of a major release. Document versions are usually used for minor releases. Users should take special note or action when using a document information record with a revision level.

3.6.7 Execute a Document Where Used

You can include a document information record in a BOM or as part of a document structure. The Document Where Used report will show you in which BOM or document structure the document information record is included. To execute this report, follow the menu path: ENVIRONMENT • DOCUMENT WHERE USED.

3.6.8 Create a Document Structure

You can create a document structure or a document BOM. This functionality is used mostly when interfacing a CAD system that has an assembly structure, such as CATIA V5 or UG NX, to SAP DMS. This assembly structure will be maintained via a document structure. When working with a CAD system interfaced to SAP DMS, special functionality in the CAD Desktop (Transaction CDESK) is provided for managing document structures associated with the assembly structure of a CAD application.

To create a document structure, follow the menu path: ENVIRONMENT • DOCUMENT STRUCTURE • CREATE. You'll be taken to the initial screen for Transaction CV11 (Create Document Structure). Here you'll verify that you want to create a document structure for the selected document information record. Press Enter, and add the document information records to the table. This is very similar to building a regular material master-based BOM.

3.6.9 Copy an Original File to a Local Directory

At times, you'll want to copy an original file associated with a document information record to your local machine. You can use this functionality when you're not checking out the file for change but simply need a local copy. To do this, select the original file and choose ORIGINALS • COPY TO. After you select the file, you'll be asked to identify where you want to store it on your local machine.

3.6.10 Reset Check-Out

If you've checked out an original file, you might at times want to cancel the check-out. You may need to do this, for example, because the locally checked-out file has been corrupted and can't be stored back into the system. To reset the check-out, select the original file, and follow the menu path: ORIGINALS • RESET CHECK OUT. The padlock icon associated with the original file will close to indicate that the check-out has been cancelled.

3.7 Product Structure Browser

Earlier in this chapter, you learned how to link a document information record to another SAP object, such as the material master. The SAP Product Structure Browser (Transaction CC04) takes advantage of these object links. The Product Structure Browser is an excellent tool for consumers of information. A *consumer* searches for information but does not create it. For example, imagine you're on the manufacturing floor and need access to all drawings for a product you're building and for which you only know the material master number. In Transaction CC04, you can execute a search by the material master number, and the following information is returned (see Figure 3.26):

▶ All documents linked to the material master

▶ The BOM associated with the material master

▶ A WHERE-USED LIST to identify in which assemblies this material master is used

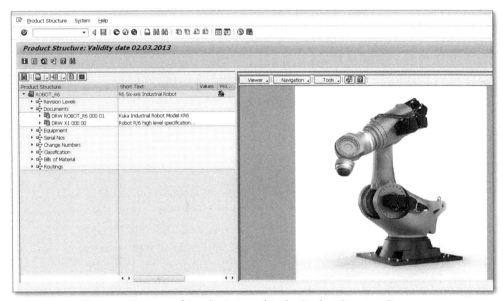

Figure 3.26 View of Results Returned in the Product Structure Browser

Also shown in Figure 3.26 is the capability to directly view original files associated with document information records. In some cases, many document information records will be linked to a material master. With this capability, you can quickly view the original files associated with multiple document information records.

Information returned isn't limited to showing the relationships among material master, BOM, and documents. As shown in Table 3.4, a lot of data can be returned if maintained, making the Product Structure Browser a "one-stop shopping" type of transaction for consumers of data.

Relations among SAP Objects Shown in the Product Structure Browser		
Document	Document Revision	Change Number
Change Notification	Material	Material Revision
Material Specification	Equipment	Functional Location
Class	Characteristics	Configuration Definition
Configuration Folder	Baseline	BOM
BOM Item	Task List	Sequence
Operation	Material Inspection Characteristic	Distribution Order
Distribution Order Packages	Recipients	iPPE Nodes
Component Variant	iPPE Alternative	

Table 3.4 Relations Shown in the Product Structure Browser

3.7.1 Select the Focus of the Product Structure Browser

In the Product Structure Browser, you can select a variety of focuses to specify how you want to view information. As an example, if you select a focus of DOCUMENT, the report will be run with the document information record as the top information item and everything else displaying below it. As shown partially in Figure 3.27, focuses are selectable via correspondingly named tabs, including MATERIAL, DOCUMENT (document information record), CHANGE NUMBER, CHAR. (characteristic), CLASS, EQUIPMENT, FUNCTIONAL LOCATION, and CONFIGURATION DEFINITION.

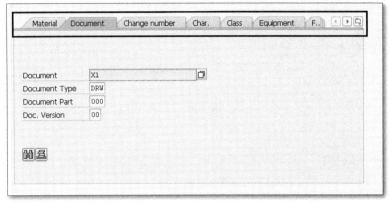

Figure 3.27 Focuses for Executing the Product Structure Browser

To show you how it works, if you run a search with the document information record as the focus, the results returned will be similar to what is shown in Figure 3.28.

As demonstrated, the Product Structure Browser is a powerful tool and can make finding information very easy. You'll see through project experience that it's a tool users appreciate because of its ease of use and the amount of information displayed.

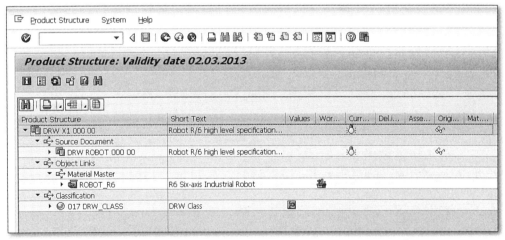

Figure 3.28 Results Returned in the Product Structure Browser When Focusing on a Document Information Record

3.8 Classification Search

The attributes on the ADDNL DATA tab of a document information record are added through the use of a default class. The creation and change process of this class is managed through functionality provided by the SAP Classification System. In Chapter 4, you'll learn how to create a class. Right now, you'll learn how to search using the classification search Transaction CL30N (Find Objects in Classes). Although Transaction CV04N (Find Document) offers similar functionality, it's important to gain some familiarity with the underlying technology that supports these attributes.

3.8.1 Example Classification Search

For the example classification search, you'll search for document information records you created in the earlier exercises. This exercise assumes that you used document type DRW to create your example document information records.

To execute a classification search, open Transaction CL30N. As shown in Figure 3.29, enter a CLASS of "DRW_CLASS" and a CLASS TYPE of "017". The class CL001 is the default class associated with document type DRW. The CLASS TYPE 017 is the class type that is associated with document information records. All classes you create for classifying document information records should belong to this class type. Press ⏎.

Executing Transaction CL30N

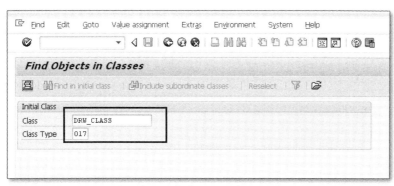

Figure 3.29 Entering the Class and Class Type for Searching

On the next screen, you'll see the characteristics associated with the class. Enter your search criteria in the characteristics on which you want to search, and click on the FIND IN INITIAL CLASS button. This executes the search. As shown in Figure 3.30, the search results are returned.

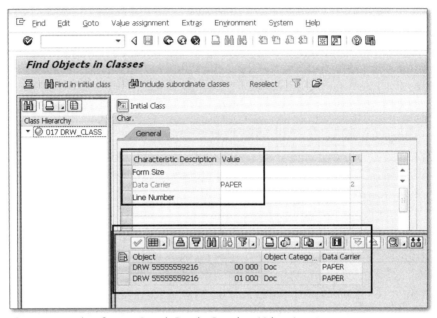

Figure 3.30 Classification Search Results Based on Values Input

In summary, the classification search capability is another tool you can use to search for documents.

3.9 Document Distribution

Through the document distribution function, you can distribute original files associated with a document information record. You can start a distribution through Transaction CVI8 (Start Document Distribution) or directly from the search results of Transaction CV04N (Find Document). This functionality is best demonstrated through Transaction CV04N because you'll often want to distribute originals associated with a set of document information records. As an example, you might want to distribute all original files associated with document information records that are linked to a certain material or engineering change.

To start a distribution through Transaction CV04N, first enter your search criteria and execute. As shown in Figure 3.31, select the document information record you want to distribute, and then select the menu item EXTRAS • START DISTRIBUTION.

Executing Transaction CV04N

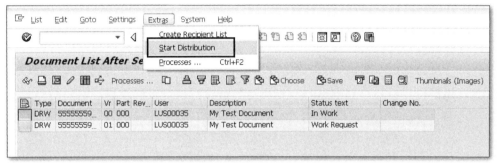

Figure 3.31 Start Document Distribution

As shown in Figure 3.32, create a recipient list on the START DISTRIBUTION screen. This can consist of internal users or external email addresses. If you want, you can keep the DISTRIBUTE IMMED. checkbox selected. If so, the distribution of the original file will start immediately on execution of the distribution.

Creating a recipient list

On execution of the distribution, the original files are collected together and sent in an email to the users specified in the recipient list. The distribution order is also assigned a number, and history or reporting on distributions is possible through Transaction CVI9 (Distribution Log).

This is the simplest type of distribution order, but you can have other types of distributions as well, such as sending via fax or copying original files to an external server.

3 | SAP DMS Step-by-Step Instructions

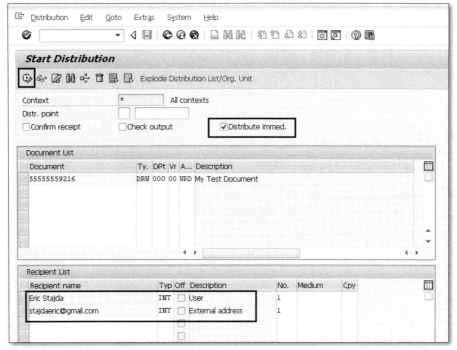

Figure 3.32 Entering a Recipient List and Starting a Document Distribution

3.10 Internal Viewer

SAP provides you with an internal viewer to view graphic and other types of files. Use of the internal viewer saves the user from launching into a separate viewing application when displaying original files, thus providing a better user experience. The internal view works with the SAP GUI. When using SAP PLM 7.01 or above, SAP provides the SAP Visual Enterprise Viewer as a viewer. This viewer provides similar functionality to the SAP GUI internal viewer but also supports more advanced processing of 3D files generated out of the SAP Visual Enterprise Generator. The SAP Visual Enterprise Generator will take your 3D CAD and turn it into lightweight 3D models that can be manipulated in the SAP Visual Enterprise Viewer or via other tools such as the SAP Visual Enterprise Author.

As shown in Table 3.5, a number of 2D and 3D formats are supported with the internal viewer. The SAP Visual Enterprise Viewer also supports many of the same formats, in addition to other formats such as the RH format (right hemisphere format), which is generated out of the SAP Visual Enterprise Generator.

Format	Description
2D vector images files	AutoCAD DWG 2.5-14 (DWG)
	AutoCAD DXF R11-14 (DXF)
	AutoCAD DWF (DWF)
	Computer Graphics Metafile (CGM)
	Initial Graphics Exchange Specification (IGES)
	HPGL/HPGL-2 (HPG, HPGL)
	HP ME 10/30 MI (MI)
	Calcomp (906, 907)
	CALS MIL-R Type I and Type II (MLR, MIL, MILR)
2D raster image files	Tagged Image File Format: monochrome, color, and grayscale (TIF)
	Windows Bitmap (BMP)
	JFIF Compliant (JPG, JPEG)
	Portable Network Graphics (PNG)
	EDMICS C4 (C4)
	(TLC)
	CompuServe (GIF)
	MIL-RII – TRIFF (FSX)
	SunRaster (RAS)
	PICT-Macintosh Paint (PCT, PICT)
	PC Paint (PCX)
	Microstation (DGN)
2D ASCII and PostScript files	ASCII Text (TXT)
	PostScript I, II (PS)
	Encapsulated PostScript (EPS)
3D models	Direct Model (*.jt)
	Virtual Reality Modeling Language (*.wrl)
	Stereolithography (*.stl)

Table 3.5 Formats Supported by Internal Viewer

When you set up application types during the configuration process, you decide if the internal viewer will be used for a specific file type. This setup is covered in Chapter 4. As shown in Figure 3.33, when displaying an original file, the file will show in the internal viewer if it's configured to do so.

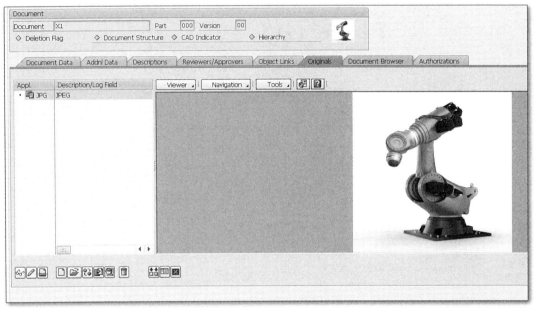

Figure 3.33 Display of a File in the Internal Viewer

Beyond viewing files, the internal viewer offers a number of additional tools:

- Navigation options, including zoom, zoom area, center, and align
- Redlining of images
- Measurement tools
- Comparison of layers
- Printing directly from the viewer

Redlining tool   One of the most useful tools from this list is the redlining tool. This tool allows users to make annotations or markups on a graphic image, which is often helpful in communicating changes that are required during an update or review process.

3.11 Summary

In this chapter, we've covered how to execute SAP DMS transactions, including the transactions to create, change, and display document information records. We also covered the Find Document transaction, which includes multiple methods for searching for documents such as searching by linked objects and full-text searching. Beyond the basic operations, we covered functionalities such as how to copy a document information record and how to execute a document where used. These functionalities are important as you begin to grow your knowledge and become more advanced in your use of SAP DMS.

We also introduced both the internal viewer and the SAP Visual Enterprise Viewer, which is used in SAP PLM 7.02. We talked about similarities in capabilities between the two viewers, as well as some differences, including the use of RH files with the SAP Visual Enterprise Viewer. We also looked at two additional transactions, the Product Structure Browser and the Find Objects in Classes transactions. It's important that you spend some time executing the transactions in this chapter before proceeding with the configuration of the system.

In the next chapter, you'll learn how to configure SAP DMS.

In this chapter, you'll learn the basic SAP DMS configuration, including the concepts and steps necessary to configure number ranges, document types, lab offices, and several other configuration items.

4   Configuring SAP DMS

This chapter shows you how to configure SAP DMS by discussing the configuration items most relevant to helping your project succeed. After you've performed these configurations, you'll be able to fully utilize SAP DMS. This includes creating document information records using your own document types and creating your own searchable attributes. All other items in this book build on the information presented in this chapter, including setting up security profiles and possibly developing workflows that can be started for specific document types and statuses.

4.1   Questions to Answer before Starting the Configuration

Make sure that you've spent a significant amount of time answering the questions presented in Chapter 2 before starting with the configuration of SAP DMS. You'll need to take the answers to those questions and turn them into configuration values. As an example, in Chapter 2, you were asked to define which documents you want to manage with SAP DMS. Based on the answer to this question, you must now think about what document types you'll create, what the status network will be for the document type, and what attributes will be associated.

In this chapter, we'll provide you with an explanation for each configuration item, and—when available—best practices for completing the configuration.

4.2 SAP DMS Configuration in the SAP IMG

The entire SAP DMS configuration is completed by configuring settings in the SAP IMG (Transaction SPRO), following the path SAP CUSTOMIZING IMPLEMENTATION GUIDE • CROSS APPLICATION FUNCTIONS • DOCUMENT MANAGEMENT.

Under this IMG path, you can configure settings for generating new document types, defining number ranges, setting up lab offices, defining revision levels, and using a variety of other options.

4.3 Configuration Steps

Completing the SAP DMS configuration follows a set of individual configuration steps that have a logical flow. This flow takes into consideration dependencies between configuration activities, and it's best to follow the flow when going through the configuration for the first time. Later, you can use this section as reference when making adjustments to your configuration.

4.4 Defining Number Ranges

The first step in the configuration is defining number ranges to be used for document information records because when you create a document information record, it's assigned a number. You'll now decide what numbers and ranges of numbers are allowed. This is the first configuration step because during the next step—defining document types—you'll use these number ranges.

To define number ranges, follow the IMG path: DOCUMENT MANAGEMENT • CONTROL DATA • DEFINE NUMBER RANGE FOR DOCUMENT NUMBERS.

Internal and external number ranges

As shown in Figure 4.1, SAP has provided you with a base set of number ranges to work with. There are two types of number ranges, internal and external. An *internal* number range is used by the SAP system for assigning document information record numbers. An *external* number range is available for users to assign document information record numbers to document information records. You can identify external number ranges by the checkmark in the EXT checkbox.

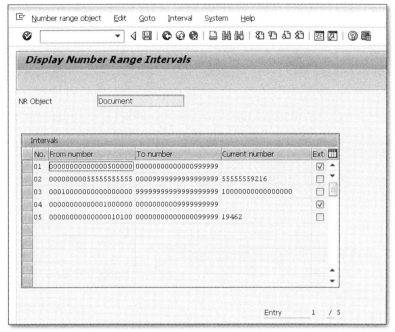

Figure 4.1 Internal and External Document Number Ranges, Delivered by SAP

If the out-of-the-box number ranges meet your number range requirements, further configuration isn't required.

New number ranges are often defined so that a document information record can receive a shorter number. If you use the SAP-delivered document number ranges, your document information records for document types using internally assigned numbers will receive a number such as "10000000240". This is typically not welcomed by users because of the length of the number. Depending on the number of document information records being stored in the system, you might consider a number range of 1000000–9999999. This is much shorter and enables you to store millions of documents using internal number assignment.

If you require a new number range, click on the INTERVAL button. A popup screen appears where you can enter a new number range. Enter the following information:

- A number identifying the number range
- A FROM value
- A TO value
- Whether the number range should be used for external assignment

When defining new intervals, you must make sure they don't overlap with currently defined number ranges. If necessary, adjust the current FROM NUMBER and TO NUMBER values to not interfere with your new range.

Number ranges can also be deleted by selecting a range and clicking on the "-" (DELETE INTERVAL) button in the main toolbar.

4.5 Creating Document Types

The most important configuration item is setting up the document types that will be used. The document type is a highly visible element to users and this is the first thing they select when creating a document information record. The document type also has a lot of attached functionality, including the following:

- Status networks
- Additional attributes used for searching
- Rules around object linking
- Conversion processes for creating neutral files
- Security rules

Much thought needs be given to defining what document types you need. In Chapter 2, we talked about defining the documents you need to manage with SAP DMS. It's now time to turn the answer to that question into document types. Let's work with an example scenario in which you have chosen to manage the key engineering documents. They fall into the following categories:

- Specifications
- Test reports
- CAD drawings
- Customer requirements

You could simply create a new document type for each of these categories. But before you do this, try to answer the following questions for each category. Based on how you answer the questions of status network, searching, object links, security, and so on, you'll have different document types. This helps you define what document types you'll require.

Defining document types

- What is the status network?
- How do you want to search?
- What objects should you be able to link to?
- Are there different security requirements?

You might find that for the document category "specifications," you want to search by specification type. This would be an additional attribute on this document type. Searching by specification type would not, however, be relevant to the document category "test reports." For test reports, you might have a different set of attributes that are needed for searching. Based on different requirements, such as additional attributes, you'll have different document types. You may also have different security requirements specifying that only a certain group of individuals can see documents that are in the category of "customer requirements." In addition, you might also want to control that customer requirements can only be linked to a customer object in SAP. This would not be the case for CAD drawings because they are only linked to the material master object.

In general, best practice is to keep the number of document types you create to a manageable number. Although it's easy to create a lot of document types, this can create a very long and confusing list of document types from which users have to choose.

For example, let's assume that the categories "specifications" and "test reports" have a lot in common; that is, they have the same search attributes, status work, security requirements, and object links. Therefore, you can create a document type of "ZSR" (Eng. Specs/Reports) for both categories. The other two categories do not have much or anything in common; therefore you can create two separate document types "ZCD" (CAD Drawings) and "ZCR" (Customer Requirements) for the two categories.

4.5.1 Configuration Location

To create document types, follow the IMG path: DOCUMENT MANAGEMENT • CONTROL DATA • DEFINE DOCUMENT TYPES.

4.5.2 Configuration Example

You'll now configure the system based on the example category "specifications," discussed previously. You'll create a document type of "ZSR" with a description of "Eng. Specs/Reports." This document type will have a very simple status network only be able to be linked to a material master. You'll also define three additional attributes for the document type: the specification/report type, the associated project, and a characteristic indicating whether the document is a controlled document requiring approval for release.

4.5.3 Configuration Steps

The document type configuration consists of the following four steps:

1. Create the initial document type.
2. Define the status network.
3. Define which object links are relevant for the document type.
4. Create a class using SAP Classification to support additional attributes.

Step 1: Create the Initial Document Type

Select the configuration item DEFINE DOCUMENT TYPES to begin the configuration. On the first screen that appears, click on the NEW ENTRIES button. This initiates the creation of the new document type. On the screen that appears, enter values and settings to define the document type. The available values and settings are defined in Table 4.1 and Table 4.2.

Table 4.1 shows document type attributes that define how the document type will function in the system. For each attribute, a brief description and a value for the example scenario are provided.

Attributes Area		
Field	**Description**	**Value**
DOCUMENT TYPE	A high-level classification that categorizes documents.	"ZSR"
DOC. TYPE DESC.	The document type description.	ENG. SPECS/ REPORTS
USE KPRO	Identifies whether original files will be checked into a KPro Content Server.	checked
STATUS CHANGE	Specifies whether the status of the document information record must be changed when a field is updated.	unchecked
REV. LEV. ASSGMT	Indicates whether revision levels can be assigned to a document information record when associating a change master.	checked
VERSION ASSGMT	Controls automatic version assignment.	checked
ARCHIVING AUTHORIZATION	Specifies whether original files associated with a document information record can be archived.	unchecked
CHANGE DOCS	Indicates whether change documents should be created when a document information record is changed.	checked
CM RELEVNCE	Determines whether the document type is controlled by configuration management.	unchecked
NUMBER ASSGMT	Controls what type of number assignment will be allowed for the document type.	"1"
INTERNAL NUMBER RANGE	Specifies which number range will be used for internal assignment.	"05"

Table 4.1 Attributes for the Document Type Configuration

Attributes Area		
Field	**Description**	**Value**
EXTERNAL NUMBER RANGE	Specifies which number range will be used for external assignment.	blank
NUMBER EXIT	Specifies the program that controls number assignment and versioning for document information records. The default is MCDOKZNR.	MCDOKZNR
VERS. NO. INCR.	Identifies which increment will be used for version assignment.	"1"
ALTERNATIVESCREEN	The number of the screen that replaces the standard system screen for the document type (program SAPLCV110; screen 0102).	blank
AScEx.	The name of the program in which form routines for the PBO (process before output) and PAI (process after input) time point of an alternative screen are stored.	blank
FILE SIZE	The maximum original file size to be stored in the SAP database. This setting is only relevant when not using the KPro Content Server.	"0"
CLASS TYPE	The class type for the default class to be assigned to the document type. The typical setting is 017.	blank
CLASS	The default class to be assigned to the document type. Fields in the class will display on the ADDITIONAL DATA tab of the document information record.	blank
DEFAULT APPL.	The default workstation application that is set when creating original files.	blank
DIS. WS APPLIC.	The application that is copied as the default value for the distribution.	blank

Table 4.1 Attributes for the Document Type Configuration (Cont.)

In Table 4.2, you'll find example values for the fields on the document information record. For each field, you can specify that it should be suppressed, for display only, an optional entry, or required.

This functionality is very useful when you want to suppress or hide fields that aren't relevant to your business requirements. For example, if you don't intend to use Engineering Change Management on document information records, you can suppress the CHANGE NUMBER field to make it invisible to users. As mentioned, you can also make certain fields required, such as adding a description to the document information record. Suppressed fields are indicated by a "–" symbol, and required fields are indicated by a "+" symbol.

Suppressing or hiding fields

Field Selection Area	
Field	**Value**
CLASS DATA	blank
HIERARCHY INDICATOR	–
DOCUMENT STATUS	blank
DOCUMENT DESC.	+
USER	blank
AUTHORIZATION GROUP	blank
LAB/OFFICE	+
CHANGE NUMBER	blank
CAD INDICATOR	–
SUPERIOR DOCUMENT	–
WS APPLICATION 1	blank
WS APPLICATION 2	blank
CM RELEVANCE	–

Table 4.2 Field Selection for the Document Type Configuration

Given the settings in Table 4.2, the fields DOCUMENT DESC. and LAB/OFFICE are required entries. The fields HIERARCHY INDICATOR, CAD INDICATOR, SUPERIOR DOCUMENT, and CM RELEVANCE are suppressed or hidden.

4 | Configuring SAP DMS

After all values have been entered, the configuration of your document type ZSR should look like Figure 4.2. You should save your work by clicking on the SAVE icon before moving on to the next step.

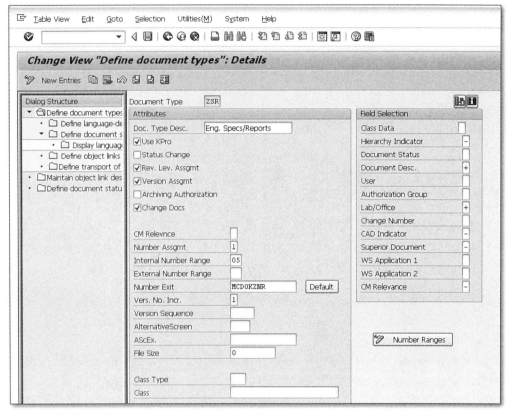

Figure 4.2 Defining Document Type ZSR

Step 2: Define the Status Network

The next step is defining the status network for the document type. As discussed earlier, you'll define a simple status network for the new document type ZSR. Specifically, a document information record of document type ZSR will start with an initial status of "In Work" and will then be allowed to proceed to a status of "Request Approval." From "Request Approval," it can move back to "In Work" or to a status of "Completed." The status of "Completed" signifies that the document information record is released, and you can assign a revision level if you desire.

With the document type ZSR open, in the DIALOG STRUCTURE pane, select the configuration item DEFINE DOCUMENT STATUS. Select the NEW ENTRIES button, which initiates adding a status to the status network. On the next screen, enter the value "IW" (for In Work) in the field DOCUMENT STATUS. You can also use the dropdown list next to the field to select the value. Next, you need to start setting the attributes for the status, which are described in Table 4.3. The value for the example scenario is also provided in Table 4.3.

Attributes Area		
Attribute	Description	Value
OBJECT CHECK	Confirms that the object link a user enters exists. For example, if a user attempts to link a document information record to a material master, the system checks to make sure the material master exists.	checked
RELEASE FLAG	Indicates whether a version of a document information record is released. Controls assignment of revision level to the document information record.	unchecked
CONTENT VERSION	Indicates whether a content version is created for an original file associated with a document information record each time it's stored.	checked
CHECK IN	Indicates whether files are automatically checked in when the status is set.	unchecked
COMPLETE FOR ECM	Shows that a document with this status is "completed" for Engineering Change Management purposes.	unchecked
DISTR. LOCK	If set, document information records with this status are not distributed via Application Link Enabling (ALE).	unchecked
CHECK-IN REQUIRED	Indicates whether all original files associated with the document information record must be checked in before the status can be set.	unchecked

Table 4.3 Attributes for the Document Type Configuration

Attributes Area		
Attribute	**Description**	**Value**
FLD SEL.	Determines whether a status log entry is required, no entry, or optional.	"-" (no entry)
STATUS TYPE	Enables you to select the status type. For this example scenario, you are selecting "I", which means that this will be the initial starting status for the document information record. Other status types are available, including temporary, locked, and archived. The locked status will be used later so that no further changes can be made to the document information record.	"I" (Initial)
PREV. 1 – 6	These fields are where you build the status network. In this case, you'll set the status of "RA" as a previous status. This indicates that you can move back to the In Work status from Request Approval. (When we get to defining the next status of Request Approval, the In Work status will be the previous status for Request Approval.)	"RA" (Request Approval)
WORKFLOW TASK: OBJECT TYPE/ OBJECT ID	The workflow definition that is triggered when the status is set.	blank
PROGRAM EXIT	The custom program that is executed when the status is set.	blank
FORM ROUTINE	The subprogram to be executed from a program as soon as a document information record with this status is saved.	blank
SIGNSTRAT.	The digital signature strategy that is executed when the status is set.	blank

Table 4.3 Attribute Settings for the In Work Status (Cont.)

When you're done, your ATTRIBUTES settings for the In Work status should now look as they do in Figure 4.3. Click on the SAVE button to save your entries.

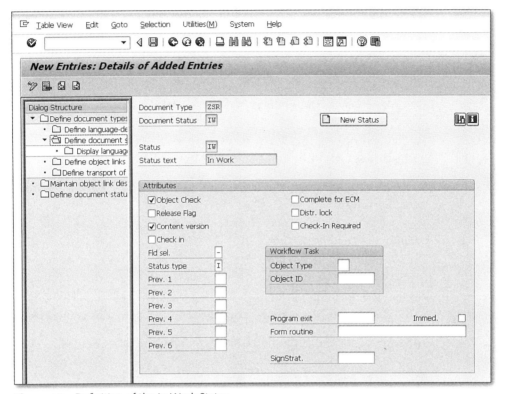

Figure 4.3 Definition of the In Work Status

The next step is creating the additional statuses of "Request Approval" and "Completed." Click on the NEXT STATUS button, and use the blank entry screen that displays to begin working.

Defining the Request Approval Status

The "Request Approval" status will follow the "In Work" status. It signals that you're requesting document approval. During approval, the document should be locked for changes.

The settings for the "Request Approval" status are outlined in Table 4.4.

Attribute	Value
DOCUMENT STATUS	"RA"
OBJECT CHECK	checked
CHECK IN	checked
FLD SEL.	"-" (no entry)
STATUS TYPE	"S" (Locked)
PREV. 1	"IW" (In Work)

Table 4.4 Attribute Settings for the Request Approval Status

The key setting here is PREV. 1. By setting it to "IW" (In Work), you're indicating that you move from the status of "In Work" to "Request Approval."

When entries are complete, save your settings and continue defining the next status.

Defining the Completed Status

The "Completed" status should follow the "Request Approval" status, and it will be the final status in the status network. When set, this status signifies that the document information is complete and released. No updates to the document information record are allowed after this status is set.

The settings for the "Completed" status are outlined in Table 4.5.

Attribute	Value
DOCUMENT STATUS	"CP"
OBJECT CHECK	checked
CHECK IN REQUIRED	checked
COMPLETE FOR ECM	checked
RELEASE FLAG	checked
FLD SEL.	"-" (no entry)
STATUS TYPE	"S" (Locked)
PREV. 1	"RA" (Request Approval)

Table 4.5 Attribute Settings for Status Completed

After your entries are complete, click on the SAVE icon to complete the building of the status network. The configuration of your status network should now look as shown in Figure 4.4.

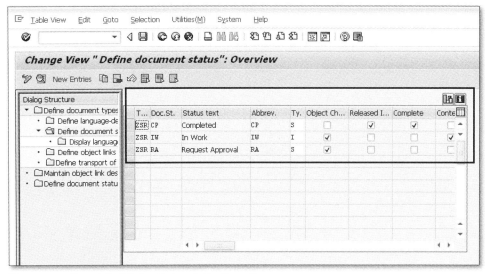

Figure 4.4 Completed Status Network Configuration

If you create a document information record using document type ZSR, the status network graphic will look like the one shown in Figure 4.5. You can review the status network from the document information record via the menu path EXTRAS • STATUS NETWORK.

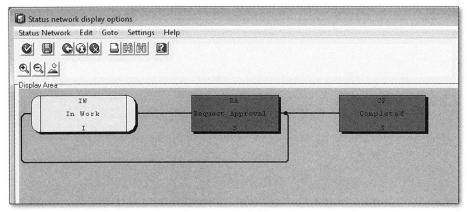

Figure 4.5 View of Completed Status Network

Step 3: Define Object Links

As shown in Table 4.6, you can link document information records to many SAP objects. Object links are powerful because they make document information records visible in many different transactions across the SAP system.

Objects		
ENGIN. CHANGE MGMT	FUNCTIONAL LOCATION	CASE
ASSET MASTER RECORD	APPROPRIATION REQ.	QUALITY NOTIFICATION
CLAIM	MEASURING POINTS	ORGANIZATIONAL UNIT
PROD.RESOURCES/TOOLS	OBJECT LINK	PATIENT
cPROJECTS ELEMENTS	REF. LOCATION	PACKING INSTRUCTION
DOCUMENT INFO RECORD	CLASS	MAINTENANCE NOTIFIC.
PURCHASE REQ. ITEM	CUSTOMER	PPE NODE
PURCHASE ORDER ITEM	VENDOR	PRODUCTION ORDER
EQUIPMENT MASTER	MATERIAL MASTER	PPE VARIANT
SUBST.REP.GEN.VAR.	PLANT MATERIAL	WBS ELEMENT
SUBSTANCE MASTER	MATERIAL COMPONENT	QM INFO RECORD
NOTIFICATION	SERVICE NOTIFICATION	LAYOUT AREA
INSPECTION METHODS	BOM HEADER	LAYOUT MODULE
QM INFO RECORD: SD	MATERIAL BOM	SALES DOCUMENT ITEM
EQUIP. REQ. (RMS)	BOM ITEM	BASELINE
PROCESS (RMS)	SAP EIS: MASTER DATA	CONFIGURATION FOLDER
RENTAL UNIT	ROOM	WCD ITEM
LEASE	MANAGEMENT CONTRACT	WORK APPROVAL
ASSET GROUP	NETWORK	LAYOUT AREA ITEM
REAL ESTATE	REQUEST	WCD ITEM
BUILDINGS	WORK CLEARANCE DOC.	WORK APPROVAL

Table 4.6 Possible Object Links for a Document Information Record

As a simple example, you'll configure the document type ZSR so that a document information record of this type can link to a material master.

With the document type ZSR open, in the DIALOG STRUCTURE pane, select the configuration item DEFINE OBJECT LINKS. Next, click on the NEW ENTRIES button.

As shown in Figure 4.6, enter "MARA" in the OBJECT field, and save the change. This is the only configuration required to link a document information record of type ZSR to a material master. If you want, you can add a few other objects to link to. Simply click on the NEXT ENTRY button, and select a new object to link to.

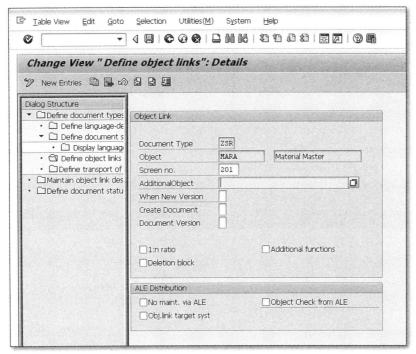

Figure 4.6 Defining an Object Link for Material Master

Step 4: Create a Default Class for Additional Attributes

In the next step, you'll create a default class for the additional attributes on this document type. As mentioned earlier, the three additional attributes are specification/report type, associated project, and a characteristic indicating whether the document is a controlled document requiring approval for release.

The creation of the default class is completed via Transaction CL02 (Class Maintenance). As shown in Figure 4.7, on the initial screen of this transaction, enter a CLASS name of "ZSR_CLASS" and a CLASS TYPE of "017". Click on the CREATE button to begin entering the characteristics.

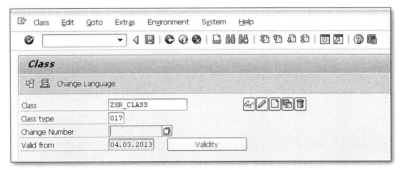

Figure 4.7 Entering Class Name and Class Type in Transaction CL02

On the next screen that appears, enter a class description of "Default Class for Document Type ZSR" in the BASIC DATA area. Next, select the CHAR. tab to start defining the characteristics. You'll create three characteristics, as described in Table 4.7.

Characteristic	Description
ZSPECREPTYPE	SPEC./REPORT TYPE
ZPROJECT	PROJECT
ZCONTROLLED	CONTROLLED DOCUMENT

Table 4.7 Characteristics to Be Created

Create a characteristic

To create a characteristic, enter the name of the characteristic, and press [Enter]. You're prompted to confirm that you want to create the characteristic. Click on YES, and on the next screen, enter the DESCRIPTION of the characteristic and a DATA TYPE. Example settings for the characteristic ZSPECREPTYPE are shown in Figure 4.8.

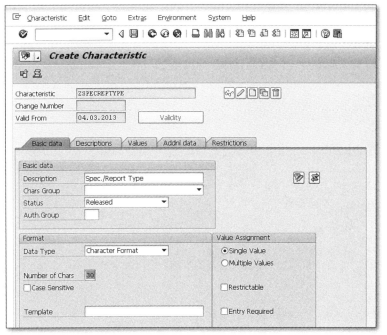

Figure 4.8 Setup of Characteristic ZSPECREPTYPE

Next, you define a set of values for the characteristic to provide users with values from which to pick. Example values are shown in Figure 4.9.

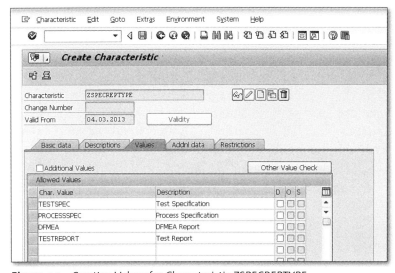

Figure 4.9 Creating Values for Characteristic ZSPECREPTYPE

Create a class After entering values, click on the SAVE button. You're returned to the main screen for adding characteristics to the class. Follow the procedure you used to create the characteristic ZSPECREPTYPE to create the characteristics ZPROJECT and ZCONTROLLED. If you want, you can vary the values allowed for each characteristic. When completed, the screen where you add characteristics to the class should look similar to the one shown in Figure 4.10. Click on the SAVE button to save the class.

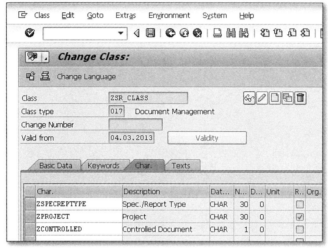

Figure 4.10 The Change Class Screen after Adding Several Characteristics Completed

The last step in this process is adding the new class as the default class for the document type ZSR. In the IMG, under the document management configuration, open the document type configuration for document type ZSR. In the CLASS TYPE field, enter "017", and in the CLASS field, enter "ZSR_CLASS". This will associate it as the default class. The results of associating this class as the default class are shown in Figure 4.11. The characteristics in the class are available for users to fill out. More importantly, they are also available to search on.

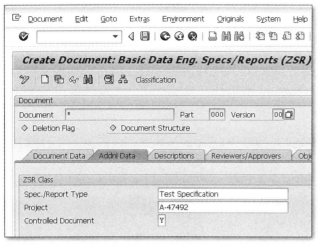

Figure 4.11 Results of Adding Class ZSR_CLASS to Document Type ZSR

4.6 Defining Laboratories/Design Offices

In this activity, you'll define the laboratories or design offices. This configuration is related to the LAB/OFFICE field on the document information record and populating the list of values available for selection by users.

> **Special Notice**
>
> This configuration also controls the configuration for the field LAB/OFFICE on the material master, which needs to be taken into consideration when updating the values.

The key thing to think about here is what you want the LAB/OFFICE field to specify or mean on the document information record and the material master. This field is often used to specify the design-responsible location or group. If it's used to represent the design-responsible location, the configuration will be populated with all of the engineering centers that exist in an organization. If it's meant to be the responsible group, it will be populated with a list of engineering groups that might be spread out across multiple locations. These are just a few ways this field can be used, but you need to clearly define what the field means in your company before proceeding with the configuration.

Lab/office field configuration

4 | Configuring SAP DMS

To define laboratories or design offices, follow the IMG path: DOCUMENT MANAGEMENT • GENERAL DATA • DEFINE LABORATORIES/DESIGN OFFICES.

As shown in Figure 4.12, this configuration activity is straightforward. You can add entries by clicking on the NEW ENTRIES button. You can delete entries by clicking on the delete button in the main toolbar. After updating the entries, click on the SAVE button.

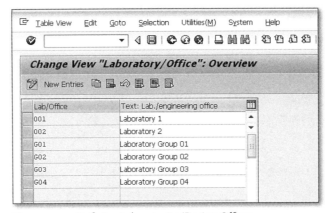

Figure 4.12 Defining Laboratories/Design Offices

4.7 Defining Revision Levels

Now you'll define revision levels that can be assigned to a document information record. Revision levels are assigned to a document information record when using a change number and specifying a status in the status network that has the RELEASE FLAG set.

As mentioned previously, revision levels are often used as an indicator of a major release. Document versions, on the other hand, are used to indicate minor releases.

To define revision levels, follow the IMG path: DOCUMENT MANAGEMENT • CONTROL DATA • DEFINE REVISION LEVELS.

As shown in Figure 4.13, the configuration activity is straightforward. You add entries by clicking on the NEW ENTRIES button, and you delete entries by clicking on the delete button in the main toolbar. After updating the entries, click on the SAVE button.

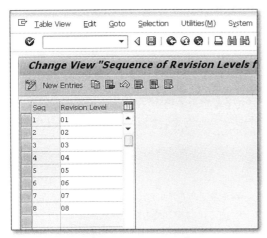

Figure 4.13 Defining Revision Levels

4.8 Defining Workstation Applications

When you store an original file on a document information record, you associate that file to a workstation application. The workstation application controls how original files are processed. More specifically, it controls which application is started when displaying or changing an original file, and how the original file is printed.

You'll define a workstation application for each application file type you want to store in SAP DMS. For example, if you want to store files generated in the application Visio, you define a workstation application that is selected when someone checks in a Visio file. The selection of the workstation application is based on the extension of the Visio file, that is, the extension VSD. You can also specify that the Visio application launches whenever someone changes or displays a Visio file that is associated with a document information record.

4.8.1 Example Workstation Application: Microsoft Word

As an example configuration, let's explore the settings for the workstation application "WRD," for Microsoft Word documents. You can then configure additional workstation applications required for your project. Beyond the workstation "WRD," SAP provides additional applications in the system from which you can learn.

4.8.2 Workstation Application Details

To execute the configuration item, follow the IMG path: DOCUMENT MANAGEMENT • GENERAL DATA • DEFINE WORKSTATION APPLICATION.

On the first screen that appears, double-click on the workstation application WRD. As shown in Figure 4.14, this takes you to the DETAILS screen where settings are configured for the workstation application.

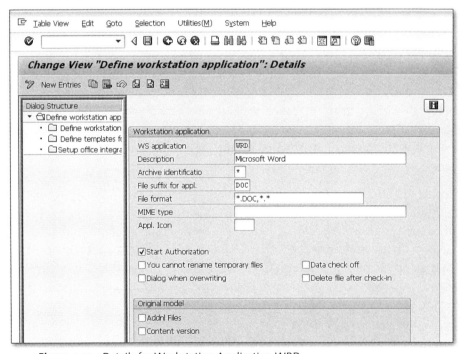

Figure 4.14 Details for Workstation Application WRD

Table 4.8 contains descriptions and sample values for each of the detailed settings for workstation application WRD.

Setting	Description	Value
WS APPLICATION	The abbreviation for the workstation application.	"WRD"
DESCRIPTION	A short description of the workstation application.	"Microsoft Word"
ARCHIVE IDENTIFICATION	The key used to uniquely identify the archive in which the original application files processed and archived with this application are stored.	"*" (You can select any of the defined archives.)
FILE SUFFIX FOR APPL.	The suffix added to the original files when processing. This includes the change and display processes.	"DOC"
FILE FORMAT	The file extensions that are relevant to the workstation application. The workstation application will be suggested when an original file with the extension is stored.	"*.DOC, *.*"
MIME TYPE	The HTML content type.	blank
APPL. ICON	The icon that will be displayed in the document information record next to the stored original file.	blank
START AUTHORIZATION	Indicates whether the application can be started.	checked
YOU CANNOT RENAME TEMPORARY FILES	When displaying an original file, this indicator determines whether the file can be renamed.	unchecked
DIALOG WHEN OVERWRITING	If set, a warning dialog appears to confirm that you want to overwrite a file if it already exists on the local machine.	unchecked

Table 4.8 Attributes for the Document Type Configuration

Setting	Description	Value
DATA CHECK OFF	Indicates whether the system checks for the existence of original files that are processed with this workstation application in the given path.	unchecked
DELETE FILE AFTER CHECK-IN	Specifies whether files on the local machine are deleted after storage has occurred.	unchecked
ADDNL FILES	If this indicator is set, you can store additional files associated to the original file with each original file. As a result, when checking out an original file, the additional files are included.	unchecked
CONTENT VERSION	Indicates whether content versions are allowed for the workstation application. If set here and in the status network, a content version is created each time the original file is updated.	unchecked

Table 4.8 Details of Workstation Application WRD (Cont.)

4.8.3 Define Workstation Application in Network

With the workstation application WRD selected, in the DIALOG STRUCTURE pane, open the configuration item DEFINE WORKSTATION APPLICATION IN NETWORK. During this step, you'll define how the application launches when displaying or changing an original file associated to the workstation application. For each data carrier, you can have three application types or actions that can be configured:

- Display
- Change
- Print

This is illustrated in Figure 4.15.

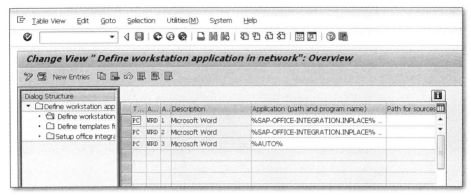

Figure 4.15 Definition of Workstation Applications in Network for Different Data Carriers

The key setting you need to be concerned with on the DETAILS screen for a specific data carrier and application type is the PATH AND PROGRAM NAME field.

In most cases, you'll use the value "%AUTO%" for this field. This allows Microsoft Windows to automatically locate the correct program when displaying or changing the original file. If required, you can also hard-code the path to the application that is launched.

Using Microsoft Office Integration

SAP provides integration to Microsoft Office products when viewing or changing these types of files. Therefore, if you use the value "%SAP-OFFICE-INTEGRATION.INPLACE%" in the PATH AND PROGRAM NAME field, Microsoft Word will be opened directly in the SAP GUI when processing original files associated with this workstation application. Additional options are available when using this integration and are best explained through [F1] help.

Using the Integrated Viewer for Graphics Files

As mentioned previously in this book, SAP provides you with an integrated viewer for multiple graphic file types, including 2D and 3D formats. To use this viewer, you can fill in the value "EAIWeb.webviewer2D.1 %SAP-CONTROL%" in the PATH AND PROGRAM NAME field. Additional options are available when using the integrated viewer and are best explained through [F1] help.

4.8.4 Define Templates for Original Files

You can define templates to use to generate new original files for a document information record. This is helpful when you want to use standard templates, such as report formats, for the generation of new original files. The definition of a template is shown in Figure 4.16. In this screen, you first specify the values for DOCUMENT TYPE, APPLIC. (application type), LANGUAGE, and NO (template number). These settings associate the template to the document type and workstation application. You then add a DESCRIPTION and either a SOURCE FILE or SOURCE DOCUMENT information record where the template can be found.

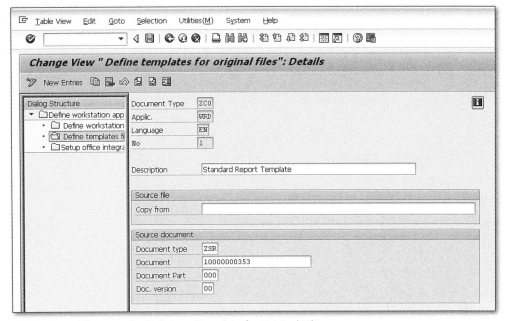

Figure 4.16 Defining a Template for Original Files

4.8.5 Set Up Microsoft Office Integration

You can set up the Microsoft Office integration so that data from the document information record is passed to the Microsoft application. This is helpful when you want to use data from the document information record in the original file. This way, the original file can be dynamically updated based on attributes stored in the SAP system.

4.9 Maintain a Default Entry for Frontend Type "PC"

To process original files correctly, you must maintain a default entry for the frontend type "PC." This specifically allows PCs that do not have the variable "HOSTNAME" set to function properly.

To configure this setting, follow the IMG path: DOCUMENT MANAGEMENT • GENERAL DATA • DEFINE DATA CARRIER.

In the configuration transaction, in the DIALOG STRUCTURE pane, select the DEFINE DATA CARRIER TYPE "SERVER, FRONTEND" item. From here, select the data carrier type PC, and select IDENTIFY FRONTEND COMPUTERS (❶), as shown in Figure 4.17. When you are on the appropriate screen, click on the DEFAULT ENTRY button (❷) to create an entry in the table with data carrier DEFAULT (❸). This is all that needs to be done. The processing of the original file should now function properly.

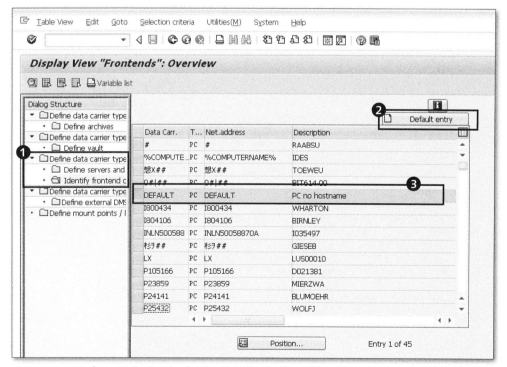

Figure 4.17 Define a Default Entry for the Data Carrier Type PC

4 | Configuring SAP DMS

4.10 Start Processing for Documents

During this next configuration step, you'll add the capability to process a set of document information records that were returned from a search using the Transaction CV04N (Find Document). Specifically, you'll add the capability to set the DELETE INDICATOR for a set of selected documents.

Document processing is carried out by selecting a group of document information records in the search results and clicking on the PROCESSES button. As shown in Figure 4.18, you can then choose from a list of functions to perform certain actions on the selected document information records. In this exercise, you'll configure the system to set up the process to set the deletion flag across multiple document information records.

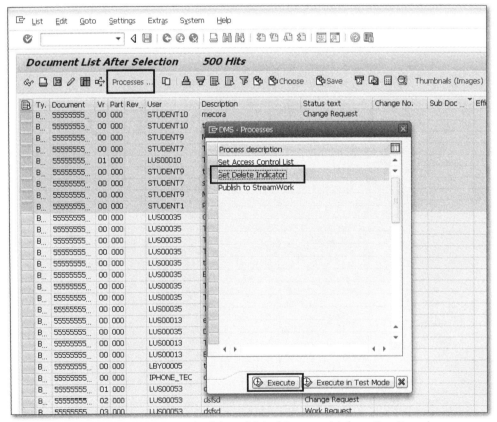

Figure 4.18 Processing the Selected Set of Document Information Records

However, this is just one example. Using ABAP, you can develop further functions to act upon document information records in specific ways. For example, you might create a function that selects a group of document information records and then executes a process that downloads all of the original files to a specific location on the user's local machine.

Function development with ABAP

To define processes, follow the IMG path: DOCUMENT MANAGEMENT • GENERAL DATA • START PROCESSING FOR DOCUMENTS.

As mentioned previously, you'll add a process for setting the deletion flag. Table 4.9 specifies the fields and values you'll use to create a new entry. Figure 4.19 shows the DETAILS screen with the fields filled out.

Field	Value
PROCESS CAT.	"Call From CV04"
DESCRIPTION	"Set Delete Indicator"
SEQUENCE	"1"
FUNCTION MODULE	"DMS_PROC_DOC_DELETE"

Table 4.9 Fields and Values to Create a Process

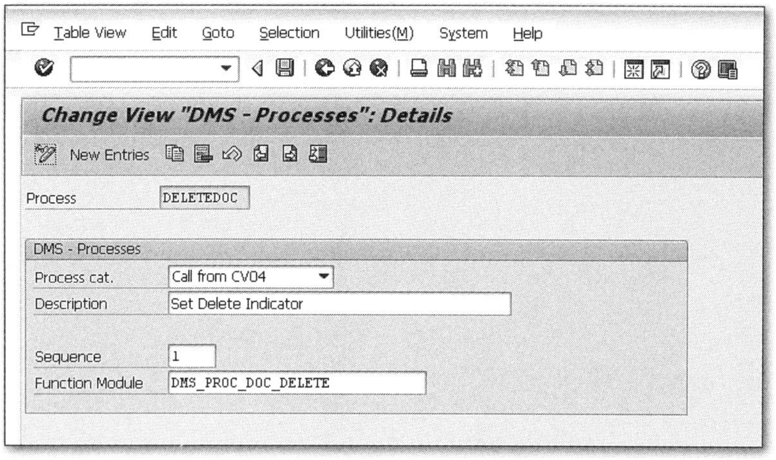

Figure 4.19 Adding Processes for Setting the Deletion Indicator

The key setting here is FUNCTION MODULE. SAP has provided the function module DMS_PROC_DOC_DELETE, which carries out setting the deletion indicator, as an example on which you can build.

4 | Configuring SAP DMS

With this process, you are only setting the deletion indicator on the selected document information records. To delete them from the system, you need to run Report MCDOKDEL in Transaction SE38.

4.11 Define Workstation Application for Thumbnails

For each document type, you can define a workstation application containing a thumbnail image that will be displayed in the document information record (see Figure 4.20). The thumbnail is displayed because an original file with application type GIF is associated to the document information record. This functionality provides users with a quick view of the original file attached to the document information record.

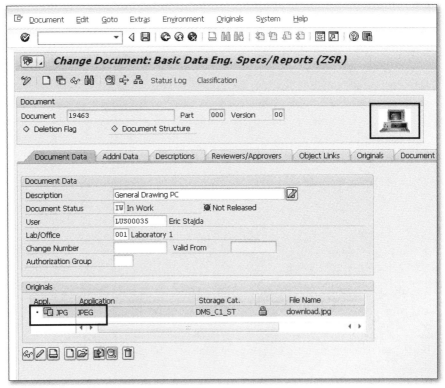

Figure 4.20 Displaying a Thumbnail in a Document Information Record

> **Added Value**
>
> If thumbnail applications are maintained, new functionality in Transaction CV04N, (Find Document) allows you to display these thumbnail images in a grid instead of a table list of document information records. Users can then search through a returned set of document information items quickly by looking at the thumbnail images.

Defining workstation applications for thumbnails is performed by following this IMG path: DOCUMENT MANAGEMENT • GENERAL DATA • SET UP WORKSTATION APPLICATION FOR THUMBNAILS (IMAGES).

To add a workstation application to be displayed as a thumbnail for a document type, click on the NEW ENTRIES button. Add the values for the fields DOCUMENT TYPE and APPLIC. (application) that you would like to use. Use only graphical applications such as applications that produce files with the GIF or JPG extension. Your entries should look as shown in Figure 4.21. When your settings are complete, click on the SAVE button.

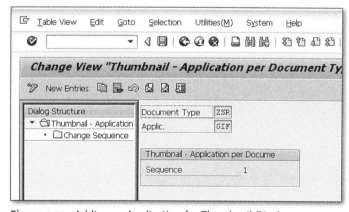

Figure 4.21 Adding an Application for Thumbnail Display

4.12 Define Profile

You can create profiles that set default values and settings for processing original application files associated with a document information record.

For each profile, you can configure the following:

- Specific users or roles that are assigned to the profile.
- Workstation applications that will start when displaying or printing original files. Also, for each application, you can configure the working directory to which you want to copy original files and a default storage category.
- A set of processes users can execute.

Using profiles is often helpful when you want to set up default applications and a default storage category for a set of users. For example, imagine that you have different applications and storage categories that users work with, based on their geographic location. Using profiles, you can set up defaults so that users don't need to make decisions about which applications or storage category to use.

To define profiles, follow this IMG path: DOCUMENT MANAGEMENT • GENERAL DATA • DEFINE PROFILE.

Steps to define a profile

The first step is creating a new profile key. Click on the NEW ENTRIES button, and enter a key and short description. Next, identify the users or roles to associate with this profile by selecting the PROFILE KEY in the right pane, and then selecting the configuration item ASSIGN GROUPS/USER TO THE PROFILES in the DIALOG STRUCTURE pane, as shown in Figure 4.22.

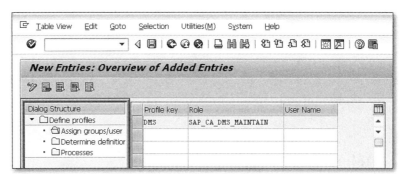

Figure 4.22 Assignment of Roles or Users to Profile

Next, select DETERMINE DEFINITIONS FOR APPLICATIONS in the DIALOG STRUCTURE pane. You'll set up default applications for printing and display.

You can also configure a default working directory and storage category for each application. Example settings are shown in Figure 4.23.

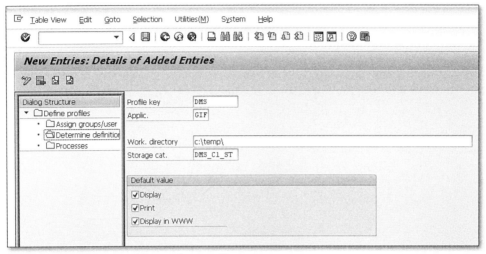

Figure 4.23 Defining Applications for a Profile

The last step is to define which processes are available to users. To add a process, select the configuration item PROCESSES in the DIALOG STRUCTURE pane, and add the processes you want to be available for the profile.

4.13 Additional Configuration Items

Additional configuration items are covered in their respective chapters. Specifically, Chapter 7 covers frontends to SAP DMS and explains how to configure web documents. Also, the configuration of items such as the content server and how to set up a conversion process are discussed in Chapter 5.

4.14 Summary

In this chapter, we covered basic SAP DMS configuration. You should now know the concepts and steps necessary to configure number ranges, document types, lab offices, and several other configuration items. With the configuration complete, you have a baseline SAP DMS in place that you can use. In terms of an actual SAP DMS implementation project, you might want to revisit the SAP DMS configuration topic throughout the life of the project. You can also start thinking about advanced topics, such as locking different frontends to SAP DMS, or enhancing the system using BAdIs and users exits.

In the next chapter, you'll learn about SAP DMS infrastructure requirements and the options for architecting an infrastructure solution.

This chapter reviews the different infrastructure components that can be deployed during an SAP DMS implementation, including content servers, cache servers, index/TREX servers, and conversion servers.

5 Infrastructure Requirements

The following four infrastructure components are part of an SAP DMS implementation:

- Content server
- Cache server
- Index server (TREX)
- Conversion server

This chapter is structured to provide you first with a general overview of each infrastructure component and to then look at the different ways to combine the infrastructure components to architect a solution. For example, a simple architecture might have one content server and one index server to allow full-text search capability. A more complex architecture might include multiple content, cache, and index servers. The architecture you end up with depends greatly on the environment in which you're implementing SAP DMS.

5.1 Content Server

The *content server* stores all of the original files that are associated with document information records in SAP DMS. When you check in an original file on a document information record, the file is taken from your local machine and stored on the content server.

The following facts about the content server are important to know:

- The content server is a separate server with its own installation of software.
- The content server can be installed on a Windows-based or UNIX-based system (AIX, HP-UX, HP-UX, Linux, and Solaris).
- The server size is based on a variety of factors, including the number of users who access the server and the number and type of documents being stored (e.g., CAD or Microsoft Office documents).
- Based on your environment's requirements, you can have one or many content servers.
- Each content server may have one or many repositories for document storage.
- You may store original files within a database or on the file system.
- If using the database for document storage, the underlying database can support up to 64TB of data.
- Installation of the content server software is a straightforward process.

> **Working without a Content Server**
>
> If you don't set up a content server, you can store originals files in the main SAP database. This happens when you select storage category DMS_C1_ST when checking in an original file. Use of the SAP database for storing files is recommended only for a small number of original files. Storing large numbers of originals in the SAP database can cause issues with system performance and backup.

5.1.1 Content Server Requests

When a user makes a request to process an original file, it goes first to the SAP system, which identifies the content server where the original file is stored. From there, the information is sent back to the client. The client, in turn, makes a request to the content server. All requests and processing of original files is handled via HTTP; therefore, a web server is set up on the content server. Storage of original files can be either in a database instance or in the file system. If using the database option, the database is known as SAP MaxDB. SAP MaxDB is the database management system developed and supported by SAP. SAP MaxDB is available on Windows, Linux, and UNIX, and for the most prominent hardware platforms. If a request has been made to process an original file, the service on the content server locates the original file and sends it back to the client. The process of locating and delivering the file to the user is mostly transparent. The user sees a status message that a file has been located and downloaded in the lower left portion of the SAP GUI.

5.1.2 Choosing Database- or File-Based Storage

As mentioned, you can store original files in either an instance of SAP MAXDB or on the content server file system. Both options work well. When evaluating which option to use, consider the following items.

- When using the file system option, at minimum, the administrator of the content server will have access to the file system and its contents. Documents can be manipulated or unauthorized access can occur. If your environment has strict security requirements, the database option will provided better controls.

- Backing up and restoring a database can be much different from backing up and restoring a file system. With a database, you can perform an incremental backup of log files and restore to the last log file in the instance of a failure. Depending on the available file system backup and restore capabilities, you may be able to restore to the last snapshot or full backup. You'll want to fully define your requirements for the backup and recovery area early in the project. This is a critical process for every SAP DMS project. Representatives from both business and IT should be a part of this discussion to ensure that all requirements and possibilities are discussed.

5.1.3 Key Transactions for the Content Server

Table 5.1 lists the key SAP transactions related to the content server. Knowing these transactions will make setting up the content server much easier.

5 | Infrastructure Requirements

Transaction	Description
CSADMIN	Content server administration
OAC0	Content repository administration
OACT	Storage category administration
SCMSMO	Monitoring for content and cache servers

Table 5.1 Key Content Server Transactions

5.1.4 Content Server Quick Installation Guide

After you've downloaded the content server software from the SAP Service Marketplace, only a handful of steps are needed for you to get the content server up and running:

1. Using the setup program, install the necessary content server software on the server.
2. In Transaction CSADMIN, link the SAP system to the content server.
3. In Transaction CSADMIN, create a repository on the content server.
4. In Transaction OAC0, link the repository to the SAP DMS.
5. In Transaction OACT, create storage categories in the repository.

You can then test the content server by storing an original file in the storage category you've configured.

5.2 Cache Server

A *cache server* is a separate server that usually resides at remote locations where no content server is installed. The goal of the cache server is to speed up access to original files for users in remote locations. The concept and use of a cache server is best explained through an example.

> **Example Cache Server Scenario**
>
> A company has an engineering facility in the United States and a manufacturing site in Romania. All of the documentation for producing the company's product is generated at the engineering facility, so a content server is installed at this location. The users at the manufacturing facility access the data generated by engineering, and a cache server is installed at this location.

> When a user at the manufacturing facility brings up a drawing of a product produced for the first time, a copy of the drawing is pulled from the content server located at the engineering facility and placed into the cache server located at the manufacturing site. The next time a user from the manufacturing location brings up that same drawing, the system first checks to see if the most recent copy of the drawing is located on the cache server before attempting to pull it from the content server at the engineering facility.

Installing one or more cache servers provides a number of benefits:

The benefits of cache servers

- Reducing access time to original files for remote users
- Reducing the use of the wide area network (WAN)
- Minimizing the required administration to maintain a cache server

If your project will have users from multiple remote locations accessing documents stored in SAP DMS, you should consider having a cache server installed at those locations.

In the next section, we'll discuss cache sizing along with how files get removed from the cache to make room for new items. Additionally, we'll look at how requests are handled to find the most optimal path for retrieving files.

5.2.1 Cache Size and Deletion

When you set up a cache server, you define the cache size. Once set, the size of the cache does not "grow" but can be increased at any time via updating the variable `MaxCacheSize` in the file *CSProxyCache.INI* on the cache server. If the cache server fills up, it will start deleting documents from the cache by performing an analysis, finding documents that have been unaccessed for the longest time, and deleting them to free up space for newer items in the cache.

In the next section, we'll discuss the logic the SAP system uses to determine the most optimal method for retrieving files based on the location of the client request.

5.2.2 Determining Path for Client Requests

The system takes the following steps to determine the best path for retrieving documents for a given client request:

1. The system establishes the location of the requesting client.
2. The system establishes the location of the content server.
3. If the requesting client and content server are in the same location, no checking for the cache server is required. The optimal path is to retrieve directly from the content server.
4. If the requesting client and the client aren't at the same location, the system will locate any cache servers at the client location.
5. If no cache servers are available at the client location, content is directly retrieved from the content server.
6. If the cache server is available, it's selected for retrieval of the document.

5.2.3 Key Transactions for the Cache Server

Table 5.2 lists the key SAP transactions related to the cache server. Knowledge of these transactions is required to configure a cache server.

Transaction	Description
SCMSHO	Define the cache server by host name and location
SCMSCA	Define the cache server by host name, port, and appropriate HTTP script
SCMSIP	Locations of IP subnets

Table 5.2 Key Cache Server Transactions

5.2.4 Customizing for the Cache Server

The following Customizing settings need to be configured when setting up the cache server:

1. Define the caches in your system:
   - Define the host name and locations (Transaction SCMSHO).
   - Define the cache (Transaction SCMSCA).

2. Define locations for the users (clients) using the following:
   - Set/get parameter LCA.
   - Host name (Transaction SCMSHO).
   - Subnet (Transaction SCMSIP). (SAP recommends that you use subnets when defining locations for users.)
3. Define the locates for the content server using the following:
   - Host name (Transaction SCMSHO). (SAP recommends that you use host names when defining locations for the content server.)
   - Subnet (Transaction SCMSIP).

You can then test the cache server by twice displaying a large original file that is stored on a remote content server. When the file is displayed the second time, access should be faster because the file is pulled from the local cache server rather than the remote content server.

5.3 Index Server (TREX)

The *index server*, or TREX, component lets you perform full-text searches on original files that are stored on a content server. For the full-text search to work, TREX makes a copy of the original files (Word, PDF, Text, etc.) located on the content server and temporarily stores them on the TREX server. An indexing process then creates a searchable index of the original files on this server. This process is similar in function to how Google and Yahoo!, for example, create a searchable index of web pages. After the index is created, you can perform full-text searches on the original files.

5.3.1 Benefits of Full-Text Searching

The main benefit for full-text searching is to provide users with another powerful tool to search for document information records. Full-text search capabilities go far beyond searching on attributes that are available on the document information record.

5.3.2 Executing a Full-Text Search

As shown in Figure 5.1, full-text searches are executed through Transaction CV04N (Find Document).

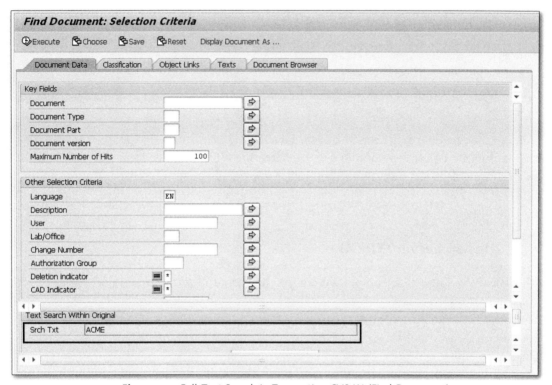

Figure 5.1 Full-Text Search in Transaction CV04N (Find Document)

As mentioned previously, full-text searching helps reduce the time users spend searching for documents. For your project, you'll need to weigh whether this will be a beneficial component to configure.

5.3.3 Use of TREX and SAP PLM 7.01

SAP Product Lifecycle Management (SAP PLM) 7.01 and future releases rely heavily on the use of TREX. Beyond indexing the contents of original files, TREX indexes the document information record attributes. (e.g., description, classification data, object links, status). The benefit of this is that you get much better search performance. This is especially critical when you're storing millions of documents in SAP DMS. Users want a Google-like search experience. This helps you come close to such performance. With this said, you're required to have an instance of TREX if you'll be using SAP PLM 7.0 and future releases.

5.4 Conversion Server

A *conversion server* carries out the process of converting original files on a document information record from one format to another. This conversion is triggered based on a status being set on the document information record.

> **Example Conversion Process**
>
> Let's look at an example where at the time a document information record reaches a status of Released, the original files that are associated with the application type WRD (Microsoft Word) will be converted to PDF and attached to the document information record.
>
> At the time of conversion, the Word files are transferred from the content server to the conversion server to be processed. When the conversion process is complete, the resulting file, in this case a PDF file, is returned to the content server and associated to the document information record.

Conversions of original files are often carried out for a variety of reasons. In the case of CAD files, the CAD data is converted to a neutral format because licenses for CAD applications are expensive, and converting CAD files to a neutral file allows others to view the data without having to use a copy of the application. Another reason is the long-term storage of documents. A PDF file is considered a long-term storage format; therefore, it's good practice to convert many types of files to PDF files so that they will still be viewable in the future, when the applications that generated the files are no longer supported.

5.4.1 SAP Software's Part in the Conversion Process

SAP provides the methodology to call a conversion process and to move the files back and forth from and to the content server. It doesn't provide the tools to perform the actual conversion on the server. For example, if you want to convert all of your CAD drawings to a neutral graphic file format such as TIF, you'll need to write a script and provide the software that can carry out the conversion. This software and the necessary scripts will reside on the conversion server.

5.4.2 Sample Conversion Scripts and Tools

SAP provides example scripts and tools for starting a conversion. As stated in SAP Help, you'll find the programs ConvUtil, ConvServSamp, and ConvRfc2Corba on the SAP server SapservX under the following path: *~ftp/general/misc/converter*.

5.4.3 Configuration of the Conversion Server

To configure a conversion server, follow the IMG path: DOCUMENT MANAGEMENT • CONVERSION OF ORIGINAL APPLICATION FILES. Then, follow these three steps:

1. Maintain the settings for the converter, including the converter destination, help program, and status.

2. Define when a conversion process is triggered and what original files should be converted.

3. Maintain location-dependent conversion data and which conversion process should be started based on the storage category or content server.

Key settings for the configuration of the conversion server

Let's take a look at a few of the key settings, starting with the document type and the document status. You can see that the conversion process will start only for DOCUMENT TYPE ZCO and when the status of the document information record is set to RL (see Figure 5.2). When these conditions are met, the converter WRD2PDF will be called. As defined in the fields APPL. (SOURCE) and APPL. (TARGET), the process will take original files of application type WRD and send them to the conversion server to be converted to type PDF.

5.5 Conversion with SAP Visual Enterprise Generator

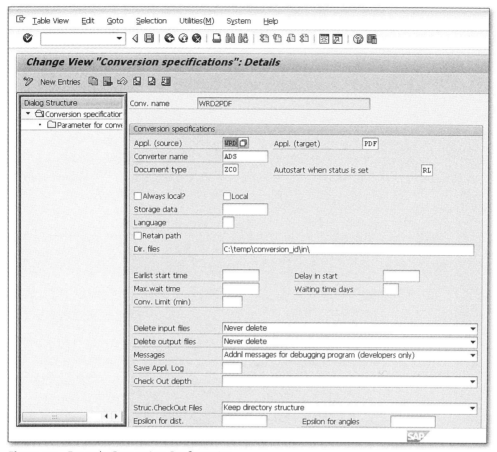

Figure 5.2 Example Conversion Configuration

A number of other settings can be configured for a conversion definition, including how to handle input and output files, specifying the earliest start time for conversion, and specifying whether there should be a delay in starting the conversion.

5.5 Conversion with SAP Visual Enterprise Generator

In a very similar manner to the conversion server, the SAP Visual Enterprise Generator allows you to translate 3D CAD files into a lightweight

The benefits of the SAP Visual Enterprise Viewer

format for downstream use, including the areas of engineering, manufacturing, and maintenance. The SAP Visual Enterprise Generator will take CAD data stored in SAP DMS and convert it into various formats such as *.rh* and *.jpg*. The converted files can also carry additional metadata, including their relationship to specific SAP data and objects. As shown in Figure 5.3, these files can then be viewed and manipulated using the SAP Visual Enterprise Viewer. There are a number of benefits, including that users are no longer required to have an expensive CAD license to access data and that converted files are much smaller and portable than original CAD files.

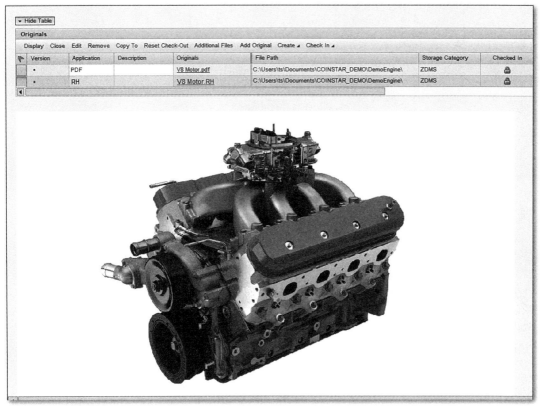

Figure 5.3 View of Lightweight 3D Model within the SAP Visual Enterprise Viewer after Conversion

Now that we've covered the basic server types, let's explore the different architecture options of these servers.

5.6 Developing Your Infrastructure Architecture

You need to think about many factors when putting together your architecture, which can consist of one or more content, cache, TREX, or conversion servers. In general, what your architecture looks like depends on three elements:

- The types of users at each location
- The functionality you're implementing
- The WAN's capabilities

5.6.1 Types of Users at Each Location

As mentioned briefly earlier in this book, two types of users exist: consumers and creators. To refresh your memory, consumers use the data that others have generated. They display this information, but they don't create new document information records. Creators, on the other hand, generate new original files and store them in SAP DMS.

For locations with a high number of creators, it's recommended that a content server is installed locally. This way, creators aren't negatively impacted by (typically slow) WAN speeds when checking in and checking out original files. Because creators are constantly working on original files, you want response times for them to be fast. Departments that typically have a significant number of creators are engineering departments because they are responsible for creating documents such as drawings, reports, and specifications.

Locations with a large number of consumers and only a small number of creators (if any) only require a cache server.

5.6.2 Which Functionalities to Implement

Let's look at some considerations as to which functionalities you should implement. If you don't plan to convert original files to a neutral file format, you don't need a conversion server. If you don't plan to have full-text search functionality or to make use of SAP PLM 7.01, you don't need a TREX server. However, if you plan to have any of these functionalities, you need to include them in your architecture. For conversion servers, you should plan to have one for each location at which you have a content server. This is especially true if you plan on performing conversions frequently because you don't want to pull original files across the WAN for each conversion. You can also have multiple TREX servers; however, in most cases, a single TREX server will suffice. This server can index the contents of multiple content servers.

We'll look at the specifics of a single content server, a single local content server with a cache, and using multiple content and cache servers.

5.6.3 Wide Area Network Capability

If you have a WAN with excellent connectivity between all of the locations, it's possible to use a single content server. However, it's more likely that you have a WAN with differing levels of service between different locations. If so, you need to implement a solution that uses multiple content and cache servers.

Let's now look at three different architecture scenarios that vary in complexity. The first uses a single content server, the second uses a single local content server with a cache server for remote locations, and the last uses multiple content and cache servers.

Using a Single Content Server

The simplest architecture includes a single content server. This can be used to support creators and consumers at a small number of locations or if the WAN supports the complete enterprise with acceptable network performance. If you plan to implement a single content server, you have to size your server appropriately for the amount of data and the number of users that will be accessing it.

Using a Single Local Content Server with a Cache Server for Remote Locations

The next level of architecture uses a single content server with cache servers at remote locations to support consumers and to help reduce access time for the remote users. The remote locations can still check in original files to the content server; however, check-in times may not be optimal because of WAN service levels between the remote locations and the content server.

Using Multiple Content and Cache Servers

If you must support multiple locations with consumers and creators at each location, you likely need a solution with multiple content and cache servers. For each location with creators, you need a content server. These locations may also have a cache server because you need to cache data coming from content servers located at other locations. You might also have sites with just a cache server and no content servers. Figure 5.4 shows a sample architecture with a content server, TREX, and conversion server located at the headquarters location, and a cache server and content server for the remote facility.

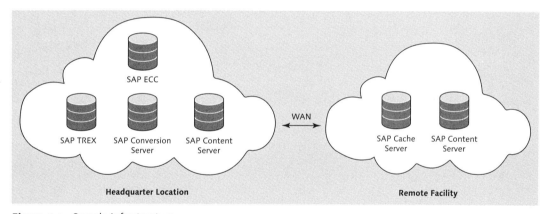

Figure 5.4 Sample Infrastructure

As you can see, many possibilities exist when you combine the different infrastructure components. Which configuration you use depends on your requirements.

5.7 Summary

In this chapter, we've reviewed the different infrastructure components that can be deployed during an SAP DMS implementation: content servers, cache servers, index/TREX servers, conversion servers, and SAP Visual

Enterprise Generator. For each infrastructure component, you learned how it works and what its purpose is, along with the steps needed to configure the component in the system. Later, you learned different ways in which the components can be deployed and what possible architectures can look like. With the information presented in this chapter, you can now start developing an architecture that will fit your environment.

In the next chapter, we'll cover the topic of setting up SAP DMS security.

This chapter reviews SAP DMS security and authorization concepts. Securing access to documents is a key component of every project.

6 SAP DMS Security

In this chapter, you'll learn about SAP DMS security and how you can use it to control access to documents. Defining and setting up your security control is one of the most important aspects of any SAP DMS project. Depending on your usage of SAP DMS, you may be storing critical and sensitive documents within the system. You'll certainly want to control and define who will have access to each and every document. SAP DMS provides you with a robust set of tools to control access to documents.

In this chapter, we'll cover standard authorization objects, non-SAP DMS authorization objects, and access control lists (ACLs). Finally, we'll look at SAP PLM 7.01 and the changes to Access Control Management (ACM).

6.1 Defining Your Security Requirements

Before discussing the technical details of document security, it's important that you first define your document security requirements. The fundamental questions are who should have access to a document, and at what point(s) in time should access be granted. Several factors will help determine the answers to these questions:

- **Customer requirements**
  If you're designing or building goods for a customer, does the customer require that you restrict access to documents that support the product?

- **U.S. government requirements, specifically military requirements**
  Are you meeting government requirements (if necessary)? For example, if you build products for the U.S. military, you must comply with

ITAR (International Traffic In Arms Regulations), which means that documents may only be shared with U.S. citizens, unless government approval is received or an exemption granted.

- **Project security**
  Should you only allow individuals involved in a project to access the related documents?

- **Patent applications**
  How do you manage access to documents that support a patent application? Should you restrict access until a certain point in the patent process is reached?

- **Financial information**
  Do documents contain financial information that if released could cause harm or hardship to the company?

- **Flexibility**
  How much effort are you willing to put into security management? Also, with each added layer of security, you must consider the cost for maintenance.

These are just a few points you need to take into consideration when defining your security requirements. Be sure to give this topic plenty of thought.

6.2 Standard SAP DMS Authorization Objects

SAP DMS comes with a number of standard authorization objects that can be used to restrict user access to document information records, by the following key attributes:

- Authorization group
- Document type
- Document status

Beyond using the standard authorization objects, you can use two additional elements to restrict access: access control lists (ACLs), and custom authorization checks using the BAdI `DOCUMENT_AUTH01`. Both of these items are covered in later sections of this chapter.

Note that authorization objects are checked in the following specific order to confirm that a user is allowed to open a document information record:

1. The SAP system checks to make sure that the user has access to execute the transaction (e.g., Transaction CV02N: Change Document).
2. C_DRAW_BGR checks access based on the authorization group maintained in the document information record.
3. C_DRAW_TCD checks access based on document type and activity.
4. C_DRAW_TCS checks access based on document type, activity, and status.
5. An ACL check is performed.
6. A custom authorization check is performed by the SAP system.

Understanding this order when setting up your security roles will make testing and verification of roles much simpler and clearer.

In the next sections of this chapter, you'll learn about the standard SAP authorization objects. Additionally, we'll cover non-SAP DMS authorization objects, including authorizations in the Bill of Materials (BOM) and classification area. A description and example usage is provided for each object.

6.2.1 Authorization Object C_DRAW_TCD: Activities for Documents

Using authorization object C_DRAW_TCD, and based on a combination of activity and document type, you can control whether a user can process a document information record. Based on the document type, you may want to restrict what actions a user can take with that document type. As an example, you may have a document type where certain users store documents and set the status on the document information record to RELEASED, which makes them official documents in your environment. Once released, they are made available for display by all. Therefore, users that create and release these documents need to have a role that allows the activity of CREATE for the specific document type. Users that display the documents need a role that allows the activity of DISPLAY.

> **Example**
>
> **Desired security:** A user should have only display access to the document type DRW.
>
> **Settings:** In the authorization object C_DRAW_TCD, the activity DISPLAY (03) and DOCUMENT TYPE DRW are maintained in the person's user role.
>
> This will give the user display access to document information records of document type DRW. No other rights will be available.

Fields, values, and descriptions for authorization object C_DRAW_TCD are shown in Table 6.1. When reviewing the table, take note of what activities are available to get an idea of how you can restrict or provide access. Think about how these activities should be combined with the document types you're using.

Fields	Values	Description
ACTVT (ACTIVITY)	01	Create.
	02	Change.
	03	Display.
	06	Delete.
	19	Maintain number range object.
DOKAR (DOCUMENT TYPE)	–	The selected activities can be executed for the maintained document types.

Table 6.1 Fields, Values, and Descriptions for the Authorization Object C_DRAW_TCD

6.2.2 Authorization Object C_DRAW_TCS: Status-Dependent Authorization

Using authorization object C_DRAW_TCS, you can control whether a user can process a document information record based on a combination of activity, document type, and status. This authorization object takes the authorization object C_DRAW_TCD and adds the element of status. You'll use this authorization object when you need to use status to restrict access or activities that can be executed.

> **Example**
>
> **Desired security:** A user should be able to access only document information records of document type DRW after they have reached a status of Released.
>
> **Settings:** In the authorization object C_DRAW_TCS, the following settings are maintained in the person's user role:
>
> - ACTIVITY = 03
> - DOCUMENT TYPE = DRW
> - STATUS = FR (RELEASED)
>
> This gives the user display access to document information records of document type DRW with a status of Released (FR). No other rights will be available.

Fields, values, and descriptions for authorization object C_DRAW_TCS are shown in Table 6.2. As with authorization object C_DRAW_TCD, you'll want to note the possible combinations of activity, document type, and status.

Fields	Values	Description
ACTVT (ACTIVITY)	01	Create.
	02	Change.
	03	Display.
	06	Delete.
DOKAR (DOCUMENT TYPE)	-	The selected activities can be executed for the maintained document types.
STATUS (DOCUMENT STATUS)	-	This is the list of statuses during/at which the user has access to perform activities against the associated document types.

Table 6.2 Fields, Values, and Descriptions for the Authorization Object C_DRAW_TCS

6.2.3 Authorization Object C_DRAW_STA: Document Status

Using authorization object C_DRAW_STA, you can define which statuses a user may set for a given document type. This authorization object is useful when you want to restrict which statuses a user can set on a document information record. As explained in the example that follows, you might, for example, want to restrict the releasing of a document information record to a specific group of individuals. This authorization object allows you to do this.

> **Example**
>
> **Desired security:** Document type DRW has a simple status network that progresses in the following manner:
>
> In Work (IW) -> Pending Approval (PA) -> Approved (AP)
>
> Any user may move the status from In Work to Pending Approval. However, only a specific group of key users may set the status of Approved. Security should restrict access accordingly.
>
> **Settings:** In the authorization object C_DRAW_STA, the DOCUMENT TYPE should be DRW, and the DOCUMENT STATUS should include IW and PA. These settings are maintained in a person's user role.
>
> This will allow the affected users to move the status from In Work to Pending Approval, but they won't have access to set the status of the document information record to Approved.

Fields, values, and descriptions for authorization object C_DRAW_STA are shown in Table 6.3. When reviewing the table, think about how you'll combine document type and document status to create the security you require.

Fields	Values	Description
DOKAR (DOCUMENT TYPE)	-	Document type to control which statuses can be set
DOKST (DOCUMENT STATUS)	-	List of statues to be allowed for the document type

Table 6.3 Fields, Values, and Descriptions for the Authorization Object C_DRAW_STA

6.2.4 Authorization Object C_DRAW_BGR: Authorization Group

Using authorization object C_DRAW_BGR, you can restrict access to document information records based on authorization group. This is often used when you want to set up project-type authorizations. As the example that follows explains, when you have groups of individuals working on projects throughout a company, you can restrict access to the documents the project groups are generating by using the authorization group.

> **Example**
>
> **Desired security:** A company has a special development project called Project 150. Only certain users should have access to the documents associated with this project. Therefore, for document information records associated with this project, the authorization group should always be set to P150.
>
> **Settings:** In the authorization object C_DRAW_BGR, the field BEGRU has the value "P150" in the person's user role.
>
> This will limit access to the document information records to those persons who have the correct authorization group maintained in their role.

The field, values, and description for authorization object C_DRAW_BGR are shown in Table 6.4. If a user should have access to an authorization group, a role for that authorization group must be created and added to the user's profile.

Field	Values	Description
BEGRU (AUTHORIZATION GROUP)	0000 – ZZZZ	Used to further restrict authorizations for document maintenance

Table 6.4 The Field, Values, and Description for the Authorization Object C_DRAW_BGR

6.2.5 Authorization Object C_DRAD_OBJ: Object Link

Using authorization object C_DRAD_OBJ, you can control the ability to add, change, display, or delete object links on a document information record for a document type at a specific status. You can use this when you want to restrict the maintenance of object links on a document information record to a certain group of individuals. This is often used because of what an object link can signify and communicate to others. Object links are visible in other transactions in the SAP system, and someone may be looking for document links to identify documents that can be used for a certain purpose.

> **Example**
>
> **Desired security:** During the lifecycle of a document information record, material masters are associated through the OBJECT LINKS tab. When the document information record reaches a status of Released (FR), no user should be able to create, change, or delete the link.
>
> **Settings:** In the authorization object C_DRAD_OBJ, the following settings are maintained in the person's user role:
>
> - ACTIVITY = 03
> - DOCUMENT TYPE = DRW
> - STATUS = FR (RELEASED)
>
> This will allow the user to display object links on the document information record. No other activities will be possible.

Fields, values, and descriptions for authorization object C_DRAD_OBJ are shown in Table 6.5. You need to identify the object link type you're working with before working with this authorization object. This is required data in the DOKOB field.

Fields	Values	Description
ACTVT (Activity)	01	Create.
	02	Change.
	03	Display.
	06	Delete.
DOKOB (Object)	-	Enter the database table for the objects here (e.g., "MARA", for material record).
STATUS (Document Status)	-	Enter the status of the document information record when object links should be controlled.

Table 6.5 Fields, Values, and Descriptions for the Authorization Object C_DRAD_OBJ

6.2.6 Authorization Object C_DRAW_DOK: Document Access

Using authorization object C_DRAW_DOK, you can grant access to display but restrict the ability to change an original file associated with a document information record. This can be used in situations where you want to grant access to change document information record data but not the associated original files.

> **Example**
>
> **Desired security:** For document type DRW, a user should have access only to display (but not change) an original file associated with the document information record.
>
> **Settings:** In the authorization object C_DRAW_DOK, the following settings are maintained in the person's user role:
>
> - ACTIVITY = 53
> - DOCUMENT TYPE = DRW
>
> This will allow the user to display any original files associated with the document information record. No other activities will be allowed.

Fields, values, and description for authorization object C_DRAW_DOK are shown in Table 6.6. When reviewing the table, pay close attention to the activities that can be restricted.

Fields	Values	Description
ACTVT (Activity)	52	Change application start
	53	Display application start
	54	Display archive application
	55	Change archive application
	56	Display archive
	57	Store archive
DOKAR (Document Type)	-	Document type to allow access to original files

Table 6.6 Fields, Values, and Descriptions for the Authorization Object C_DRAW_DOK

6.2.7 Authorization Object C_DRZA_TCD: Activities for Recipient Lists

Using authorization object C_DRZA_TCD, you can set which activities a user is allowed to perform for recipient lists. This is used when working with distribution orders.

> **Example**
>
> **Desired security:** A user requires full access when working with distribution orders.
>
> **Settings:** In the authorization object C_DRZA_TCD, activity "*" is maintained. All activities will then be available to the user when working with distribution orders and recipient lists.

The field, values, and descriptions for authorization object C_DRZA_TCD are shown in Table 6.7. Activities that can be used for restricting or granting access to distribution orders and recipient lists are identified.

Field	Values	Description
ACTVT (Activity)	01	Create
	02	Change
	03	Display
	06	Delete (only own recipient lists)
	41	Delete (administrator)
	A9	Send (start distribution with recipient list)

Table 6.7 The Field, Values, and Descriptions for the Authorization Object C_DRAW_DOK

6.2.8 Authorization Object C_DRZI_TCD: Distribution Order

Using authorization object C_DRZI_TCD, you can limit parts order processing when working with distribution orders by only allowing display of the distribution log and granting no other access.

> **Example**
>
> **Desired security:** A user should only be able to display the distribution log and have no other access.
>
> **Settings:** In the authorization object C_DRZI_TCD, activity "03" is maintained. The user will only have access to display the distribution log.

The field, values, and descriptions for authorization object C_DRZI_TCD are shown in Table 6.8. Activities that can be used for restricting or granting access to the distribution log are identified.

Field	Values	Description
ACTVT (Activity)	01	Start the distribution manually from the distribution log.
	02	Start the distribution again from the distribution log.
	03	Display the distribution log.
	04	Confirm receipt.
	05	Confirm output.
	06	Ignore distribution order.
	07	Display mail from the distribution log.
	08	Delete temporary files from the application server.

Table 6.8 The Field, Values, and Descriptions for the Authorization Object C_DRAW_DOK

6.3 Additional Non-SAP DMS Authorization Objects

The authorizations objects described in Section 6.2 relate specifically to the SAP DMS area. You'll need to consider a few other non-SAP DMS authorization objects as well because SAP DMS touches the areas of SAP Classification and bill of material (BOM) management for document structures. The additional authorization objects to be considered are listed and described in the following subsections.

6.3.1 Authorization Object C_TCLA_BKA: Authorization for Class Type

This authorization defines access to classes via the class type. This authorization is checked in all functions that use the classification system to classify objects or maintain classes.

When processing documents, users need access to class type "017".

The field, value, and description for authorization object C_TCLA_BKA are shown in Table 6.9. These can be used for restricting or granting access to specific class types.

Field	Values	Description
CLTYP (Class Type)	CLASS TYPE	The class type a user will have access to

Table 6.9 The Field, Value, and Description for the Authorization Object C_TCLA_BKA

6.3.2 Authorization Object C_KLAH_BKL: Authorization for Class Type

This authorization group defines whether the user is allowed to allocate objects to a class. The classification authorization group allows you to restrict access to certain classes.

When you create or change a class, you can enter an authorization group for classifying objects in the class. A user can only classify objects in the class if the user master record contains the authorization group you entered. Fields, values, and descriptions for authorization object C_KLAH_BKL are shown in Table 6.10.

Fields	Values	Description
AUTCL (Authorization group for classification)	AAA–ZZZ, 000–999	Authorization group for classification.
ACTVT (Activity)	01	Maintain classification data for the specified authorization group.
	03	Display classification data for the specified authorization group.

Table 6.10 Fields, Values, and Descriptions for the Authorization Object C_KLAH_BKL

6.3.3 Authorization Object C_STUE_BER: Bill of Material Maintenance

This authorization object allows you to restrict the maintenance of BOMs. In this case, BOM maintenance is related to the creation of a document structure. The document structure is maintained as a BOM of category "D" or document.

The system checks this authorization when you call a transaction for maintaining BOMs. If the authorization group is changed while the BOM is being maintained, the system checks the authorization again. Fields, values, and descriptions for authorization object C_STUE_BER are shown in Table 6.11.

Fields	Values	Description
ACTVT (Activity)	01	Create a BOM.
	02	Change a BOM.
	03	Display a BOM.
	06	Delete a BOM.
	24	Create archive file.
	41	Delete from database.
STLTY (BOM Category)	M	Carry out defined activity for material BOM.
	D	Carry out defined activity for document BOM.
	E	Carry out defined activity for equipment BOM.
	K	Carry out defined activity for sales order BOM.
	S	Carry out defined activity for standard BOM.
	T	Carry out defined activity for functional location BOM.
STLAN (BOM Usage)	1–N	Defined as part of configuration.
BEGRU (Authorization Group)	0000–ZZZZ	Restrict access based on authorization group.

Table 6.11 Fields, Values, and Descriptions for Authorization Object C_STUE_BER

In the next section, we'll cover the use of access control lists (ACL). Using ACLs, you'll be able to define very specific security control for each individual document that goes beyond the usage of authorization objects.

6.4   Use of Access Control Lists

As of SAP ERP 2005, the use of ACLs is standard in SAP DMS. Previously, this functionality was available through the use of SAP Easy DMS. To implement ACL capabilities in earlier releases, you must follow the instructions outlined in SAP Note 798504.

Using ACLs, you can control which users, groups of users, roles, or HR objects have access to a document information record. This is an additional check on top of the checks performed through standard authorization objects.

The use of access control lists versus authorization groups

With ACLs, you can give control to a user to decide who should have access to a document information record. This is an important capability that wasn't available in earlier releases of SAP software. It's often used when working with project groups where you give a project group the ability to restrict access to the document information records they are creating without generating additional roles and going through the process of adding these roles to a user's profile. Earlier in the chapter, we discussed the use of authorization groups. This is the classic method used to fulfill this requirement. However, it has the downside that a lot of roles and user profiles must be updated. Using ACLs involves much less maintenance effort.

To further explain the use of ACLs, let's look at an example scenario.

> **Example**
>
> Joe S. is the owner of document information record 10000000315/ZCH/000/00. At this point in time, many individuals have access to this record because of the authorizations assigned in their user roles.
>
> However, access to this document information record needs to be restricted due to the nature of its content. Joe S. could create a new authorization group and request a new user role to accomplish this, but it would be much easier to add an ACL to the document information record. This way, he can specifically select which users he wants to add and what privileges they will have.

To create an ACL, he selects the AUTHORIZATIONS tab in the document information record. He is then asked if he wants to create document-specific authorizations. After answering yes, he is taken to the tab where he can start adding users, user groups, roles, and HR objects that should have access to the document information record (see Figure 6.1).

To add a user, he clicks on the plus icon in the toolbar. This inserts a new row.

For this document information record, he wants Christian H. to have Read access to the document information record. As shown in Figure 6.2, he configures the following settings to achieve the desired security:

- TYPE OF AUTH. OBJ. = USER
- ID = "LUS00001" (his user ID)
- ACTIVITY = READ

When the configuration is saved, Christian H. will have only read or display access to the document information record. If Christian attempts to enter into change mode, he will receive a message that he doesn't have the correct authorizations.

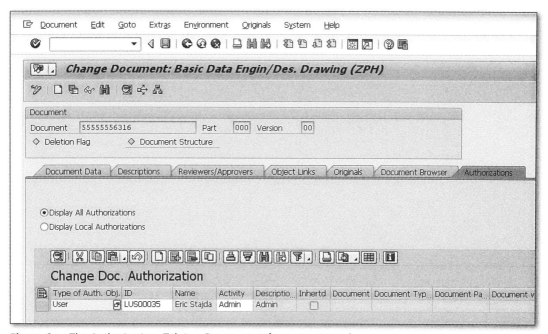

Figure 6.1 The Authorizations Tab in a Document Information Record

6 | SAP DMS Security

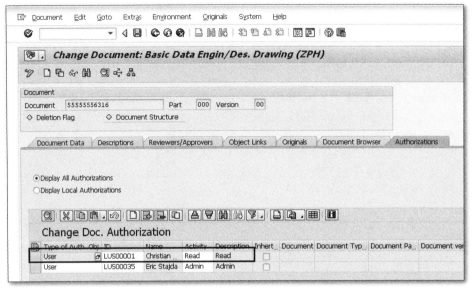

Figure 6.2 Addition of Christian H. with Read Access to Document Information

Beyond assigning a single user to a document information record, you can also assign a user group, role, or HR object.

A number of activities exist that define the level of security a user can be assigned using an ACL, as described in Table 6.12.

Activity	Description
ADMIN	Gives users full access to display, change, rename, copy, and delete documents and linked files.
DELETE	Allows users to delete a document.
WRITEFILE	Allows users to create, delete, and change originals, and to change metadata. The document can't be deleted.
WRITE	Allows users to change documents. Deletion isn't allowed. Changing a document includes editing and saving an original as well as changing the metadata.
READFILE	Allows users to display metadata and originals. The original can be exported but can't be changed or deleted.
READ	Allows users to display metadata. Changes aren't possible.
NOAUTH	No authorizations are assigned.

Table 6.12 Activities That Can Be Assigned through an ACL

Using ACLs is very helpful when you want to manage document information records at a very granular level but don't want the overhead and additional time required to generate new roles.

6.4.1 Override of ACL via Authorization Object ACO_SUPER

You use the authorization object ACO_SUPER to give certain users, such as system administrators, authorization to override the ACLs. This is required because individual administrators of documents may leave their position or company, or some other event will occur where the ACLs on a document need to be adjusted. The override allows you to carry out adjustments and avoid having orphaned documents that no one has access to.

In the next section, we cover the usage of Access Control Management (ACM), which much like ACLs, allows you to control document security to a very fine level. ACM was introduced as part of SAP PLM 7.01.

6.5 SAP PLM 7.01: Access Control Management

SAP introduced Access Control Management (ACM) as part of SAP PLM 7.01. The use of ACM allows you to control access to documents and other SAP PLM objects based on the assignment of a control context. As shown in Figure 6.3, you assign the control context on the GENERAL DATA tab of the document information record.

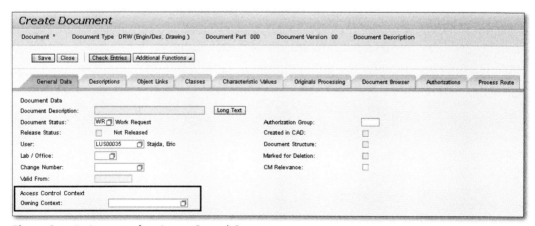

Figure 6.3 Assignment of an Access Control Context

The main benefit of using ACM is greater access control of documents and other objects within the SAP PLM 7.01 environment, which standard authorizations objects don't provide. As an example, traditional authorization objects provide you access to all documents of a specific document type. With the use of ACM, you can restrict access to specific documents within a document type in a simple fashion. It allows for greater flexibility when you need to meet complex security requirements, as often is the case in today's business world.

Configuring the access control context (ACC)

The first step in utilizing ACM is to setup your access control context (ACC). To set up a new ACC, complete the following steps:

1. From SAP PLM 7.0, select menu option CREATE ACCESS CONTROL CONTEXT.
2. On the initial screen, enter a CONTEXT NAME, select a CONTEXT TYPE, and select the PARENT CONTEXT.
3. On the GENERAL DATA tab, enter a short description for the context.
4. On the DESCRIPTIONS tab, enter any additional language-dependent descriptions for the context.
5. Click on the CONTEXT HIERARCHY tab. This tab will show any subordinate contexts to to the existing context. Because this is a new context, nothing is displayed.
6. On the ROLES/USERS tab, assign roles to the context. The role defines the type of access allowed to the object. After the roles are assigned, you then assign users or users groups to the roles.
7. The OBJECTS tab displays which objects are currently assigned to the context. Because this a new context, nothing is displayed.
8. The PROCESS ROUTE tab allows you to send your new context through a simple workflow process if desired. This is helpful when a new context should be reviewed as part of a defined business proces.
9. Click on the SAVE button. Your new context is ready to be used.

After you've assigned a control context to a document, the AUTHORIZATIONS tab will display the type of access allowed to the document, as shown in Figure 6.4.

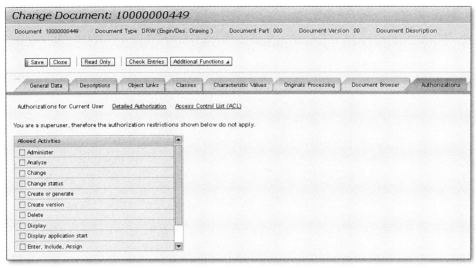

Figure 6.4 The Authorizations tab Showing the Allowed Access to a Document

ACM is another tool that can help you meet situations where you have complex security requirements that go beyond what is offered as part of the basic SAP DMS authorization objects.

6.6 Customer-Specific Authorization Checks

If the standard SAP authorization objects don't address all of your security requirements, you can use also use BAdI DOCUMENT_AUTH01 to add customer-specific authorization checks. You may have a specific business requirement that can only be addressed through a custom authorization check. For example, you might want to check an attribute on a material master to which the document information record is linked. If the attribute has a certain value, only certain users are allowed to view the document information record. There might be a customer table that defines the attributes and the users that are allowed to view the document information record.

You'll find further information about this topic in Chapter 11, which covers BAdIs and user exits.

6.7 Summary

In this chapter, we covered the topic of SAP DMS security. Specifically, you were asked to define your security requirements, including when and whether to allow users access to sensitive document records. You then learned about the standard SAP authorization objects—access control lists (ACLs), Access Control Management (ACM), and other methods, including the use of BAdI `DOCUMENT_AUTH01`—used to control access. Each was covered with a description and example of use. With this information, you can now develop a number of strategies to control access to documents.

In the next chapter, we'll cover the different frontends that are available for SAP DMS.

This chapter reviews the different frontends that are available for SAP DMS.

7   Frontends to SAP DMS

Several different frontends are available for SAP DMS, including WebDocuments, SAP Easy DMS, and portal iViews. A *frontend* simply provides a different view for users to perform the same activities that they would in the SAP GUI. Each frontend offers a different set of benefits and capabilities. For example, WebDocuments offers simplified access to SAP DMS through a web browser. Many users enjoy working through a web browser instead of using the SAP GUI because of the simplicity and familiarity of the browser.

All of the frontends use the same SAP DMS configuration, which is minimal. When your SAP DMS configuration is complete, you can start working with the different frontends. Let's now look at each frontend in detail.

7.1   WebDocuments

SAP provides a tool for managing document information records via a web browser, known as WebDocuments. This tool is often used when a business is looking for a user interface (UI) that is simpler than the SAP GUI. For example, your business may have a set of users who don't execute any activities in the SAP GUI beyond SAP DMS functions. Therefore, they won't need to be trained on how to use the SAP GUI and can instead get to all of the functionality they require through a web browser.

Some of the actions you can complete via a web browser using WebDocuments include the following:

- Find document information records.
- Display and edit document information records.

- Create new document information records.
- Update additional attributes, object links, and language-dependent descriptions on document information records.
- Change original files.
- Execute searches by basic document attributes, classification, full text, and linked objects.

As you can see, you can perform almost all of the actions in the web browser as you can in the SAP GUI. Actions you can't perform via web browser include displaying the status network, opening the Product Structure Browser, or displaying the change history. Even though these functions are not available, the WebDocuments application remains a very attractive tool for a certain set of users.

7.1.1 The Technology behind WebDocuments

WebDocuments is developed using Business Server Page (BSP) technology. You can review the underlying programming of the WebDocuments tool through Transaction SE80 (Object Navigator). As shown in Figure 7.1, in the navigator, select object type BSP APPLICATION and application CVAW_ENTIRE.

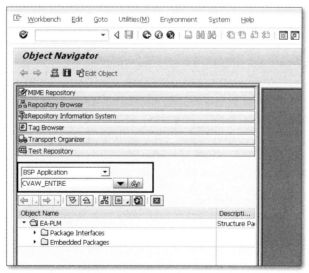

Figure 7.1 The Object Navigator

The key activity you can perform from here is launching the application. Right-click on the folder labeled CVAW_ENTIRE, and select the option TEST to launch your browser where you'll be asked to log in. Enter your user name and password. Launching WebDocuments via the Object Navigator will cut down on the time spent looking for the correct URL for the application.

7.1.2 Configuration of WebDocuments

The WebDocuments tool is configured via the SAP IMG. It's located in the same area where all other document management configuration is completed. Specifically, the configuration is completed by executing actions under SET UP WEB DOCUMENTS (BSP).

Configuration consists of two steps. First, you must define which document types you want to make available in WebDocuments. Then for each document type, make the following configurations:

1. Define the possible field groups, or sections, of the document of the information record that should be available:

    - DOCUMENT KEY
    - DOCUMENT DATA
    - ADDITIONAL DATA
    - OBJECT LINKS
    - ORIGINALS
    - DESCRIPTION

2. Define the functions that will be available to the user:

    - DISPLAY STATUS LOG
    - DISPLAY VERSIONS
    - DISPLAY HIERARCHY
    - SEND
    - DELETE
    - CREATE NEW VERSION

3. Define the thumbnail image application.

Document type configurations

Now that you're familiar with the configuration required for WebDocuments, let's take a look at an example configuration that will detail how to configure the field groups, define the functions, and define the thumbnail image application.

Example Configuration

The first item to complete is defining which document types will be available for use with WebDocuments, as shown in Figure 7.2. In the example, the document types for engineering design drawings, archive footage, specifications, and others will be available via WebDocuments.

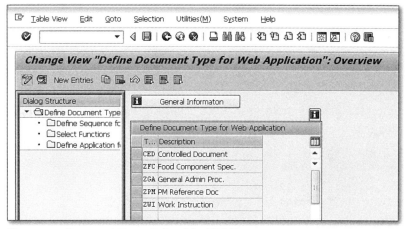

Figure 7.2 Document Types Defined for WebDocuments

Selecting the document type CED, you can drill down to review and change the sequence for fields groups, as shown in Figure 7.3. For a specific document type, you can view or specify the order for the field groups DOCUMENT KEY, DOCUMENT DATA, ADDITIONAL DATA, OBJECT LINKS, ORIGINALS, and DESCRIPTION. These relate to sections or tabs on the document information record.

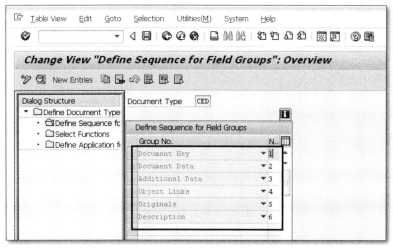

Figure 7.3 Defining the Sequence for Field Groups

You can also take a look at what functions will be available for the document type you selected, as shown in Figure 7.4. For the document type CED the functions DISPLAY STATUS LOG, DISPLAY VERSIONS, and CREATE NEW VERSION will be available.

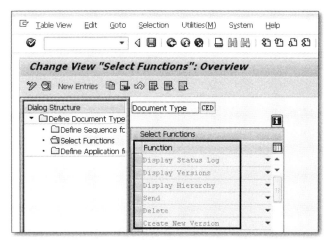

Figure 7.4 Functions Available for Document Type CED

The last item you need to configure is whether you want to define an application for thumbnails. Doing so will make WebDocuments display a small thumbnail image when one is available as an original file associated with the document information record. An example is shown in Figure 7.5.

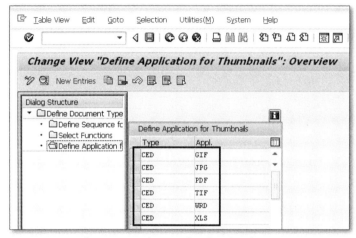

Figure 7.5 Defining an Application for Thumbnails

This completes the required configuration. You can now begin using the WebDocuments tool.

7.1.3 An Example of Working in WebDocuments

We'll now go through a simple example of working in WebDocuments by reviewing how to execute a search. After the search is complete, you'll update the document information record description and display the original files that are attached to it. Remember that this is meant to be a simple example for you to learn basic navigation and actions. When you've completed this exercise, executing additional functions will be intuitive.

Open WebDocuments and Log In

Open WebDocuments in your web browser and log in. The initial page of WebDocuments is shown in Figure 7.6. From this page, you can do the following:

- Open the stack (recent documents information records processed).
- Find document information records.
- Open past search results.
- Display or change a specific document information record.
- Create a new document information record.

For this example, click on the FIND link located in the toolbar on the left side of Figure 7.6.

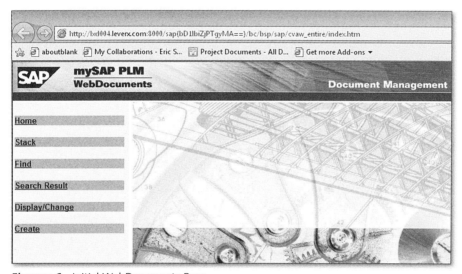

Figure 7.6 Initial WebDocuments Page

On the search screen, as shown in Figure 7.7, you can execute a variety of searches. This includes searching by basic document attributes, classification, object links, and full text.

For this example, we'll execute a search for document information records linked to a certain material master. For search criteria, select object "Material Master" in the LINKED OBJECTS SEARCH areas and enter the material number you want to search on in the material field, and then click on the START SEARCH button.

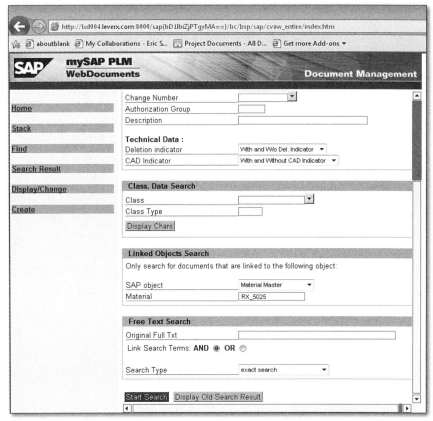

Figure 7.7 The Search Screen in WebDocuments

Next, the search results are returned, as shown in Figure 7.8. Click on the pencil icon next to the document information record you're planning to change.

As shown in Figure 7.9, the screen for changing the document information record appears. From here, you can change a variety of elements on the document information record. Based on the configuration you have set up, this can include the following:

- Basic data attributes
- Language-dependent descriptions
- Additional attributes
- Original files

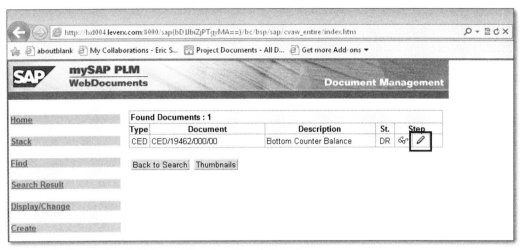

Figure 7.8 Search Results Returned Based on Search Criteria

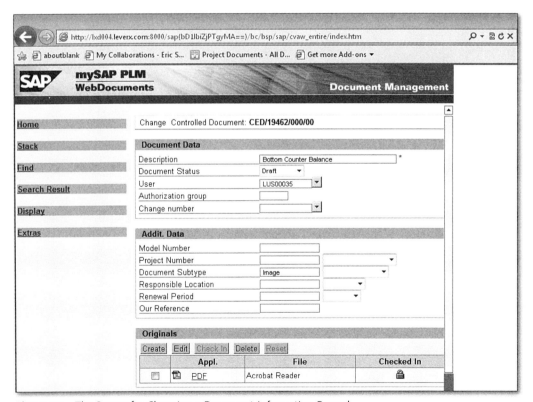

Figure 7.9 The Screen for Changing a Document Information Record

On the document information record you opened, update one of the attributes. This can be something simple, such as updating the description. When complete, click on the SAVE button to save your changes and complete the example.

As mentioned earlier, WebDocuments is an excellent tool for users who you may not want to train to use the SAP GUI. It's also a good tool to have in your arsenal of items to deploy to meet business requirements. From the standpoint of configuration and rollout, it's easy to use and has low impact.

7.2 SAP Easy DMS

SAP Easy DMS is another frontend to SAP DMS you can use. It's actually a Microsoft Windows application that is installed on a local machine. As the name states, SAP Easy DMS makes the task of managing documents easier for users by providing the following functionality:

- Check in, check out, and save documents directly in Office applications (Word, Excel, etc.).
- Use private and public folders for document management.
- Drag and drop documents to initiate document storage.
- Search for documents outside of the SAP GUI.
- Edit classification data.
- Create and edit objects links.

Users like SAP Easy DMS because they don't need to initiate an SAP GUI session to store a document. Instead, they can store documents directly from an application, such as Word, or by using the drag-and-drop functionality.

Storing a document using SAP Easy DMS

As an example of the SAP Easy DMS interface, Figure 7.10 shows the dialog box used to store a document. You can see that based on DOCUMENT TYPE, you have to fill in a certain set of fields, including the fields in the ADDITIONAL DATA area. When completed, a document information record will be created in the SAP system. The file will also be stored in the selected content server.

7.2 SAP Easy DMS

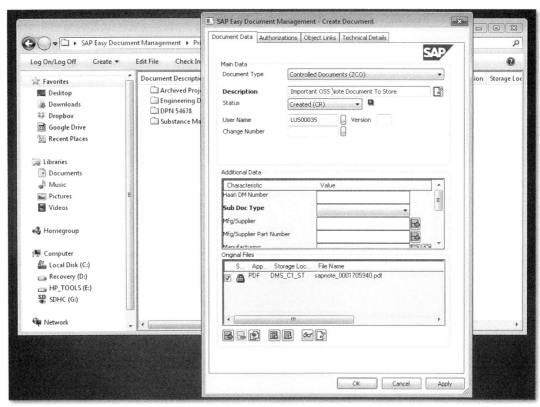

Figure 7.10 Storing a Document using SAP Easy DMS

Figure 7.11 shows a folder structure created in SAP Easy DMS. The use of folders in SAP Easy DMS is one of its main selling points and benefits because users get to work with the familiar concept of folders for organizing documents. The folder structures are actually maintained in the backend SAP system as document structures. You can view these document structures in the backend via Transaction CV13 (Display Document Structure). You also can create document structures (Transaction CV11) and change document structures (Transaction CV12). Any changes made to document structures via the SAP GUI will be reflected in SAP Easy DMS. Even with this capability, it's recommended that you stick to using SAP Easy DMS for creating and manipulating folders to start with.

SAP Easy DMS folder structure

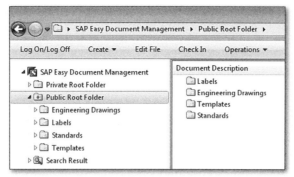

Figure 7.11 Folder View in SAP Easy DMS

7.2.1 SAP Easy DMS Installation

You can download SAP Easy DMS from the SAP Service Marketplace in the installation and upgrades area. After the download has completed, installing SAP Easy DMS is as simple as extracting the files contained in the ZIP archive and executing the setup program. After installation, you should reboot the computer.

7.2.2 SAP Easy DMS Configuration

SAP Easy DMS works with the existing SAP DMS configuration, so no additional configuration is required. When you store a document using SAP Easy DMS, you're presented with the same document types, additional attributes, and object link possibilities as if you were working in the SAP GUI.

7.2.3 SAP Easy DMS and Microsoft Windows Explorer

SAP Easy DMS integrates with Microsoft Windows Explorer to enhance its standard features for processing and managing your documents and folders. The new set of features appears after SAP Easy DMS is installed. With this concept, all features and functions of Windows Explorer are available to SAP Easy DMS users. This includes cutting, copying, and pasting. Additionally, the drag-and-drop capabilities are available for moving documents between folders and also for the initial creation of documents. Being tightly integrated to Windows Explorer is one of the main selling points for SAP Easy DMS. Most users will pick up the usage of SAP Easy DMS very quickly due to their experience of working within Windows.

7.2.4 Controlling SAP Easy DMS via Registry Settings

SAP Easy DMS provides a set of registry values that can be maintained to control the behavior of the application. These values can be set by the PC administrator at the time of installation to define behavior for all instances of SAP Easy DMS; that is, functionality can be controlled centrally. Values can also be controlled by the user.

All registry values are stored in hives, depending on the value assigned to them. SAP Easy DMS uses the following registry hives:

- **Hive Key Current User (HKCU)**
  The user has access to the hive and can make changes.

- **Hive Key Local Machine (HKLM)**
  This hive is controlled by the administrator.

> **Example Registry Setting**
>
> After editing a file, the normal process is that files are automatically checked back into SAP Easy DMS. As the administrator, you want to disable this function and have the check-in only occur when the user initiates the process. Via registry item DISABLEAUTOCHECKIN, you can set it so that files are only checked in when the user initiates the process. The value of the registry item would be "1" in this case.

7.2.5 Additional Features When Working with Files in SAP Easy DMS

When you right-click on a file in SAP Easy DMS, as shown in Figure 7.12, you'll get a list of additional actions you can take on the selected files.

Let's take a look at short descriptions of the functionality available when working with files in SAP Easy DMS:

7 | Frontends to SAP DMS

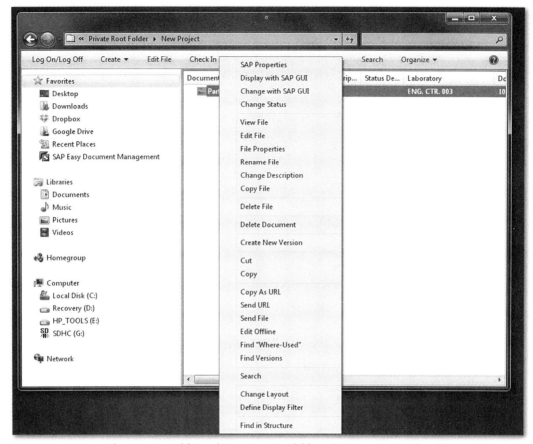

Figure 7.12 Additional Functions Available in SAP Easy DMS When Right-Clicking on a File

Additional functionality with SAP Easy DMS

- SAP PROPERTIES
  Displays the SAP properties, including description, status, owner, classification data, and authorization information. This is the SAP Easy DMS representation of the document information record.

- DISPLAY WITH SAP GUI
  Opens the SAP GUI and displays the document information record.

- CHANGE WITH SAP GUI
  Opens the document information record in SAP GUI in change mode.

- CHANGE STATUS
  Allows the user to change the status for a selected file.

- **View File**
  Opens the selected file in view mode.
- **Edit File**
  Opens the selected file in edit mode.
- **File Properties**
  Shows the Windows files properties for the selected file.
- **Rename File**
  Renames the physical file.
- **Change Description**
  Updates the description of the document information record.
- **Copy File**
  Copies the selected file to a new document information record.
- **Delete File**
  Deletes the selected file from the document information record.
- **Delete Document**
  Deletes the document information record from SAP.
- **Create New Version**
  Creates a new version of the document information record.
- **Cut**
  Removes the selected file from the folder.
- **Copy**
  Places the selected file on the Windows clipboard.
- **Paste**
  Pastes the copied file as a new document information record. This is only displayed when something is on the clipboard for pasting.
- **Copy As URL**
  Places the URL link in the Windows clipboard for the selected file.
- **Send URL**
  Opens the email program and includes a link to the selected file in an email for sending.
- **Send File**
  Opens the email program and includes the selected file in an email for sending.

- EDIT OFFLINE
  Copies the file to the local PC for editing offline.
- FIND "WHERE-USED"
  Shows all folders where the file is referenced.
- FIND VERSIONS
  Shows all versions of a selected file.
- SEARCH
  Opens the search dialog, where the user can search for documents using a variety of conditions.
- CHANGE LAYOUT
  Allows the user to change the layout of columns displayed.
- DEFINE DISPLAY FILTER
  Allows the user to filter which results are shown in SAP Easy DMS, including applying such filters as latest version, latest released, and hiding folders that empty.
- FIND IN STRUCTURE
  Finds files within a selected structure.

In addition to the action performed on a file, SAP Easy DMS also includes additional features when working with folders.

7.2.6 Additional Features When Working with Folders in SAP Easy DMS

When right-clicking on a folder, you'll find additional functions beyond the basic operations of working with files. Following are basic descriptions of these functions:

- EXPORT FOLDER
  Exports or downloads folders and contents to the local drive.
- DELETE FOLDER
  Deletes the folder from the SAP system. To delete, the folder must be empty.
- CREATE FOLDER
  Creates a new folder in the selected location.

- SYNCHRONIZE LATEST VERSION
  When working with offline folders, this function synchronizes local and SAP system content with the latest version of files stored in SAP. The synchronization function displays all conflicts between files and folders before updating and proposes solutions to conflicts.

- SYNCHRONIZE LATEST RELEASED
  When working with offline folders, this function synchronizes local content with the latest release version of files stored in SAP. The synchronization function displays all conflicts between files and folders before updating and then proposes solutions to conflicts.

- SEARCH INSIDER STRUCTURE
  Searches inside the selected folder.

7.2.7 Searching

SAP Easy DMS provides the same searching capabilities that are available in the SAP GUI Transaction CV04N (Find Document) as shown in Figure 7.13. This includes searching by document type, description, status, owner, and classification attributes. Additionally, you can restrict the number of results returned or add the results to an existing search that has been executed.

Transaction CV04N and SAP Easy DMS

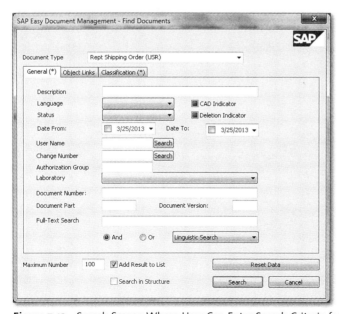

Figure 7.13 Search Screen Where User Can Enter Search Criteria for Searching

7.2.8 Editing Offline

Offline editing allows you to download a complete structure to a local directory so that you can edit it there, independently of SAP Easy DMS. When you log on to SAP Easy DMS again, the system checks for updated files and then synchronizes the local folder and SAP.

To edit files offline, when working with folders, select the option SYNCHRONIZE LATEST RELEASED or SYNCHRONIZE LATEST VERSION. The system provides a dialog box in which you can load the folder and resolve any conflicts that arise (see Figure 7.14). As mentioned earlier, the system synchronizes the offline folder with the online folder at every login. Therefore, the SAP system will remain in sync with your local folder.

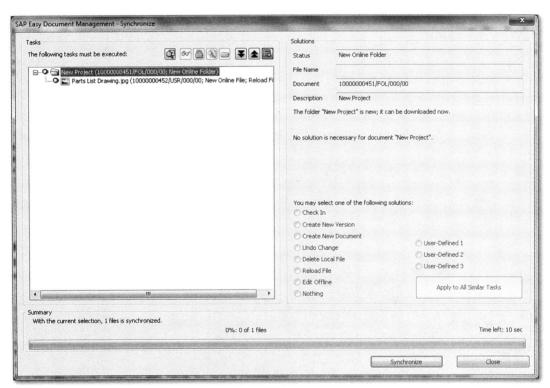

Figure 7.14 Synchronization Dialog

7.2.9 Adjusting the Layout

As shown in Figure 7.15, you can adjust which columns are shown as part of the SAP Easy DMS display. The DOCUMENT DESCRIPTION, FILE DESCRIPTION, STATUS DESCRIPTION, LABORATORY, DOCUMENT NUMBER, TYPE, PART, VERSION, USER, LAST CHANGED, and LAST CHANGED BY are shown as part of the default layout. You change this layout to include fewer fields or add additional fields. Some additional fields you may want to include are authorization group, change number, and storage location. You may also adjust the order of the columns using the common MOVE UP and MOVE DOWN functionality.

After you have a layout that you like, you can save it as variant. You can also make one of the variants as the standard layout or global layout for all users. Use of global layouts can be helpful to ensure that all users are seeing the same layout. This is something you'll want to think about prior to the roll-out of SAP Easy DMS.

Using variants for an SAP Easy DMS layout

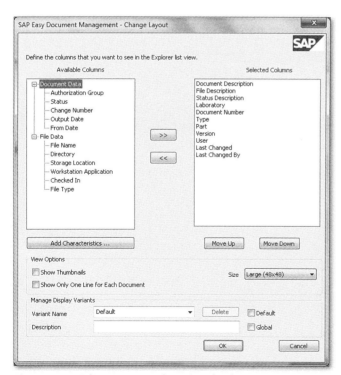

Figure 7.15 Adjust Layout and Displayed Columns

7.2.10 Using Filters

As shown in Figure 7.16, you can define display filters or conditions in SAP Easy DMS that will control which documents are shown to the user. Filter options include showing only the latest version or latest released, hiding folders without files, and hiding documents without files. Additionally, you can set up very specific filter criteria to filter on document types, owner, status, and so on. The possibilities are limitless. This allows you to narrow down and only present the documents that are relevant to the user. After a filter has been set up, it can be saved and set as a default. Additionally, you can set a global filter that applies to all users.

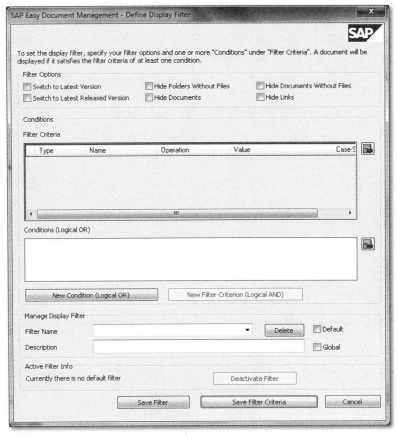

Figure 7.16 Set Filters for Display of Documents

7.2.11 Effort for Implementing SAP Easy DMS

Because SAP Easy DMS uses the backend SAP DMS configuration, the actual effort for rolling out SAP Easy DMS as an application is relatively straightforward. As long as SAP DMS is configured as you want it, you can immediately begin using SAP Easy DMS. Most of the effort is then spent on the business rules of how the tool should be used and how folders should be structured. Additionally, you should consider whether you'll make use of the additional authorization capabilities and filters, and if you want to present a global layout of columns to the user. As discussed, training should be light because users are very familiar with working with Windows Explorer, which SAP Easy DMS mimics in many of its functions.

7.3 SAP DMS Portal iView

You can use the SAP portal to access documents that are managed by the SAP system. Specific iViews are provided with the business package mySAP ERP DMS Connector for Knowledge Management (KM). The benefit is that you can add this functionality as additional information that you're able to access via your portal. The portal is meant to be the one place users can go to for information, instead of having a wide variety of websites and applications to navigate.

System requirements

The system requirements for using the business package for SAP DMS are as follows:

- **Portal**
  SAP NetWeaver 2004 (stack 10) or SAP NetWeaver 7.0 (or later)
- **Backend system**
  SAP R/3 (release 4.6C and later) or SAP ERP ECC 6.0
- **Other**
  Plug-In 2003.1 (or later)

7.4 Summary

In this chapter, we covered three different frontends to SAP DMS:

- The WebDocuments web-based UI
- The SAP Easy DMS Windows application
- The SAP DMS portal iViews to make SAP DMS visible in your portal

These frontends are often helpful when you need to provide users with a different entry point into SAP DMS other than through the standard SAP GUI. Each frontend has its own benefits and capabilities, and is relatively simple to get up and running. It's important to remember that the frontends use the existing SAP DMS configuration. Therefore, when you've completed your SAP DMS configuration, it's possible to immediately begin working with the different frontends. In some cases, you may consider using many different frontends depending on your user base.

In the next chapter, you'll learn about SAP PLM 7.02 DMS Web UI.

This chapter introduces you to the SAP PLM DMS Web UI, including its history, capabilities, how to use it, and how to configure SAP PLM 7.02.

8 SAP PLM 7.02 DMS Web UI

In this chapter, you'll learn about the new SAP PLM 7.02 web user interface (Web UI). We'll discuss the history of this interface, including the benefits and differences between what the Web UI and the SAP GUI. We'll then go through a simple exercise for creating a new document information record in the new Web UI. During the exercise, you'll learn about the similarities, differences, and new features of Web UI. We'll then look at some of the overall capabilities of SAP PLM 7.02, including searching, personal object work lists, and the object navigator, to give you a good background in how to use the system. We then look at new configuration items that need to be considered when using the Web UI.

8.1 Introducing the New Web UI for SAP DMS

As part of SAP PLM 7.0, a new web user interface (Web UI) was introduced for the SAP PLM product. The overall goal of SAP PLM 7.0 and future releases is to improve usability and offer enhanced functionality. When working with the new Web UI, you'll notice that navigation between SAP objects and data is greatly improved. You no longer have to jump between transactions. All key data is connected via links and can be quickly accessed.

SAP DMS falls under SAP PLM, so the DMS functions were included as part of the new PLM Web UI. When working with the new SAP DMS Web UI, you'll notice a great deal of similarities with the capabilities offered in the SAP GUI. Many of the capabilities are exactly the same, but there are new functions as part of the Web UI that aren't reflected back in the SAP GUI (e.g., process routes). Additionally, you'll find some items that you can get to only when working with the SAP GUI. (e.g., change documents) The nice thing is that you can quickly navigate from the Web UI to the backend SAP GUI transaction via a link. With this in mind, all information is quickly accessible when working with the new Web UI.

In the next section, we'll cover working with the Web UI, logging in, and creating a new document information record in the Web UI which will demonstrate how you can use the new interface.

8.2 Working with the SAP PLM 7.02 DMS Web UI

As a simple exercise, let's walk through the process of creating a new document information record in the SAP PLM 7.02 DMS Web UI. During this exercise, we'll take a look at the similarities and differences when compared to SAP GUI. This will provide you with a good feel for what is possible (e.g., ability to use Access Control Management) and what you need to be aware of when moving to this release of SAP PLM. (e.g., process routes are only available in the Web UI). We'll look at the process holistically starting from logging into SAP DMS via SAP NetWeaver Business Client (NWBC). We'll then explore how to create documents and review each component in more detail.

8.2.1 Logging Into SAP PLM 7.02 DMS via SAP NetWeaver Business Client

To access the SAP PLM 7.02 DMS Web UI, you'll log in via the SAP NetWeaver Business Client (NWBC). NWBC is available as a fully installed piece of client software just like the SAP GUI, or it can be accessed by running Transaction NWBC from the SAP GUI. Having NWBC and basic SAP PLM 7.02 configuration are requirements to access the SAP DMS Web UI. SAP provides a master guide for configuration and setup of SAP PLM 7.02 and NWBC on the SAP Service Marketplace. Look in the RAPID DEPLOYMENTS SOLUTION area for PLM in the Service Marketplace. You'll find many of the key documents here.

8.2.2 Create Document

After you've logged into NWBC, you'll notice a menu item for Documents. Click on this menu item, and a set of Services appears. For SAP DMS functions, you have the three basic functions of Create, Change, and Display, as shown in Figure 8.1. For demonstration, we'll create a new document information record in the SAP DMS Web UI. First click on Create Document under the Services menu item.

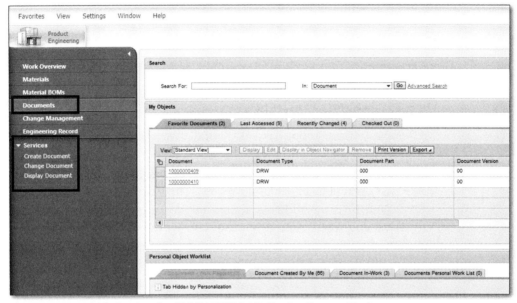

Figure 8.1 Available Services for SAP DMS Web UI: Create, Change, Display

On the Create Document screen that appears as shown in Figure 8.2, you can enter your document number, part, and version. Additionally, you have the option of copying from an existing document information record. This is very similar to working with the SAP GUI. As shown in Figure 8.2, select Document Type DRW or Eng./Design Drawing as an example. Click on the Continue button.

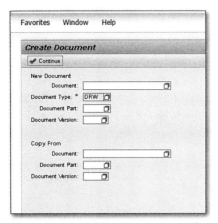

Figure 8.2 Initial Creation Screen in the SAP DMS Web UI

8.2.3 Populate General Data

After the initial creation screen, the full document information record appears as represented in the SAP DMS Web UI. As shown in Figure 8.3, the GENERAL DATA tab is very similar to what is presented in the SAP GUI document information record. The main difference in the SAP DMS Web UI is the ability to assign the document information record to an owning access control context (in the OWNING CONTEXT field). As discussed in Chapter 6, Access Control Management (ACM) allows you to control access and authorizations for a specific document at a very detailed level. This is very useful when you have a document that contains specific intellectual property or other key information that you want to allow only a small subset of individuals to access. Besides the OWNING CONTEXT field, you should find the remainder of the GENERAL DATA tab very familiar at this point.

Descriptions

Within the DESCRIPTIONS tab in the CREATE DOCUMENT window, shown in Figure 8.4, you can assign additional language-dependent descriptions to the document information record. This is the same capability as offered in the SAP GUI. The benefit of additional language-dependent descriptions is that users who log in to the SAP system in a variety of languages can see descriptions that match their language selection.

8.2 Working with the SAP PLM 7.02 DMS Web UI

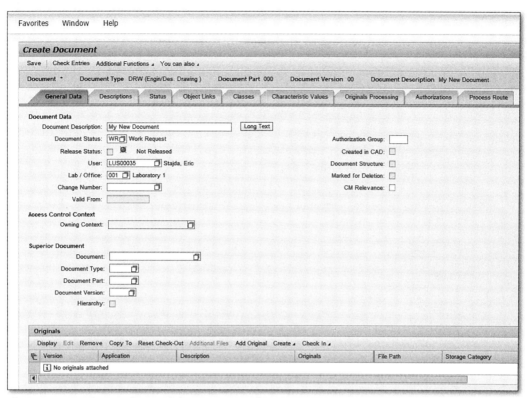

Figure 8.3 Initial General Data of the Document Information Record

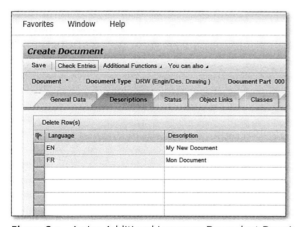

Figure 8.4 Assign Additional Language-Dependent Descriptions

Status

As shown in Figure 8.5, the STATUS tab shows the current status of the document information record and history of who and when a specific status has been set. The representation of this information in tab form is specific to the SAP DMS Web UI. In the SAP GUI, you'll find this information via a number of menu items and buttons in the document information record. The goal for the SAP DMS Web UI was to consolidate this onto one simple tab for easy access. As mentioned, you can see the current status, set the next status, and review the status history log. Additionally, you get a graphic of the status network that shows you the current status of the document information record and the next available status.

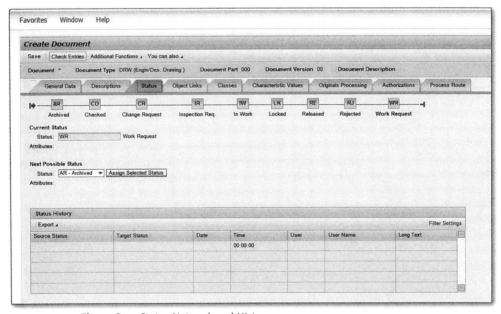

Figure 8.5 Status Network and History

Object Links

The OBJECT LINKS tab in the SAP DMS Web UI serves the same purpose as it does in the SAP GUI: enabling you to link the document information record to other SAP objects, such as the material master. The main difference you'll find is the requirement to add an object and then enter the object key. As shown in Figure 8.6, the MATERIAL MASTER object has been added, and a link has been made to a related material master. You can add one or many different object link types to a document information record. Which object links you can add depend on the underlying configuration you've made for the document type.

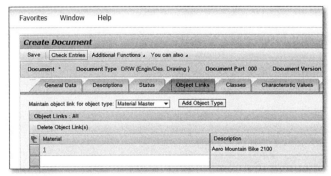

Figure 8.6 Example Object Link: Document Information Record Linking to Material Master Number 1

Classes

The CLASSES tab is specific to the SAP DMS Web UI. In the SAP GUI, this isn't represented as a tab but is accessed via a menu item. The CLASSES tab allows you to assign a class or classes to a document information record. Assignment of classes allows you to add business-specific attributes to document information records, which aid in searching and classifying documents. This capability has been described in earlier chapters. As shown in Figure 8.7, the class ZDMS_TST_CLASS has been assigned to the document information record.

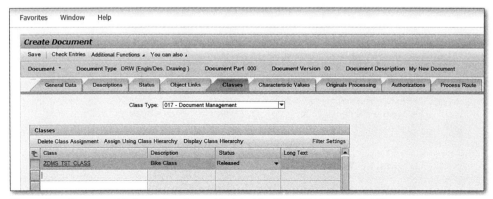

Figure 8.7 Document Information Record Related to Class ZDMS_TST_CLASS

Characteristics

The CHARACTERISTIC VALUES tab serves the same purpose as the ADDITIONAL DATA tab in the SAP GUI version of the document information record; that is, it displays the characteristics associated to the document information record. The characteristics are determined based on which class or classes are assigned via the CLASSES tab. As shown in Figure 8.8, you'll see a variety of characteristics on the CHARACTERISTIC VALUES tab due to the assignment of class. In this case, the class ZDMS_TST_CLASS was assigned, so the characteristics of this class are displayed.

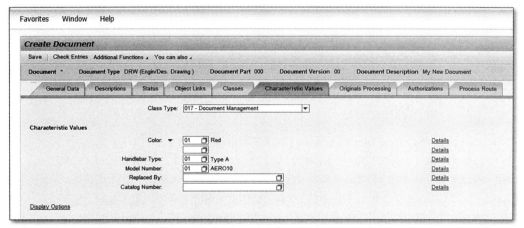

Figure 8.8 Characteristics Associated to the Document Information Record via the Assigned Class

Figure 8.9 Original Processing Tab: All Original Files Associated to Document Information Record

Originals Processing

The ORIGINALS PROCESSING tab shows all original files that are associated to the document information record. As shown in Figure 8.9, one original file is associated with the document information record. You can associate one or many original files with the document information record. From the ORIGINALS PROCESSING tab, you can also add, delete, and display the original files.

Authorizations and Access Control Management

The AUTHORIZATIONS tab shows the current authorizations you have to the document information record. This is only displayed if you've assigned an owning context to the document information record on the GENERAL DATA tab. As show in Figure 8.10, no additional information is displayed on the AUTHORIZATIONS tab because an owning context hasn't been assigned on the GENERAL DATA tab of the document information record.

Figure 8.10 Display of Additional Authorization Data

Authorizations will be shown after an owning context is assigned (see Figure 8.11).

Additionally, by clicking the DETAILED AUTHORIZATION hyperlink on this tab, you can enter a user name to determine the authorizations for that user You can also include additional authorization checks by adding to the access control list (ACL). You use an ACL to restrict or expand the activities for a user to access a single document information record. You control these activities with respect to existing ACLs. This gives you another option of further restricting access to the document. From an activity perspective, you can restrict based on the activities of change, display, delete, no authority, or granting all activities. Authorizations granted via an ACL override the restrictions from the owning context. Figure 8.12 shows the screen where you can add and manage the ACL for a given document information record.

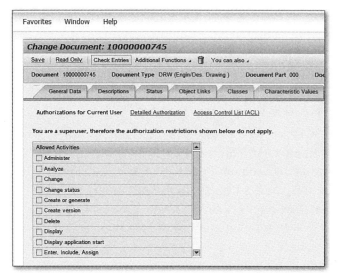

Figure 8.11 Authorization Information for the Current Document Information Record

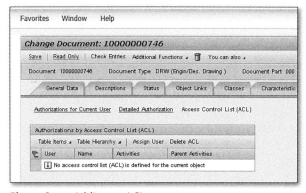

Figure 8.12 Adding an ACL

Process Routes

The PROCESS ROUTE tab is a new function available only in the SAP PLM Web UI. As a simple definition, it supports the creation and processing of workflows for the specified object. The ability to create a process route is available in the document information record, as well as in other objects (e.g., engineering record) in the SAP PLM Web UI. From a technical standpoint, the underlying technical infrastructure is based on the standard

SAP Workflow engine. Required setup and configuration to use process routes is provided in the configuration section of this chapter (Section 8.4).

Follow these steps to create a process route for the specified document information record:

Creating a process route

1. From the CREATE DOCUMENT screen, select the PROCESS ROUTE tab.

2. Enter the process route items. You can create one or many simple sequential tasks or one or many parallel tasks.

3. For each task entered, enter an agent who is responsible for processing the task along with an activity type (e.g., DISPLAY, CHANGE, REVIEW). You can also enter when you want the task completed by and a task priority.

4. After you've entered all of the steps you want in the process route, save the document information record. The START WORKFLOW button appears on the process route toolbar. When ready, click on this button to initiate the process route. When the process route is initiated, a workflow item for the first item in the process route is sent to the specified user. The next step in the process route is sent to the next user in line after the first process route item is completed.

In Figure 8.13, you see the PROCESS ROUTE tab populated with a single sequential task.

Figure 8.13 Process Route Tab

An additional feature you should take note of is the ability to save a process route as a template and also insert a saved template. You'll find this capability under the ADDITIONAL FUNCTIONS option on the PROCESS ROUTE tab. This allows you to build a standard process route of many different steps and then later reuse it by inserting the process route in

Saving a process route

other document information records. The ADDITIONAL FUNCTIONS menu is shown in Figure 8.14.

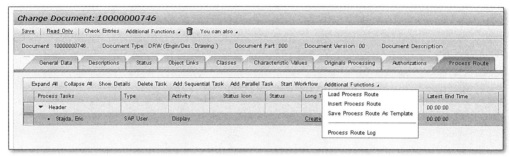

Figure 8.14 Process Route: Additional Functions Menu

Now that we've reviewed how to work with SAP PLM 7.02 DMS, let's take a look at some of the additional features of the new Web UI.

8.3 Additional Features of the SAP PLM 7.02 Web UI

In the upcoming section, we'll review additional features that are general capabilities of the SAP PLM 7.02 Web UI. This includes capabilities such as My Objects, Simple Search, Advanced Search, and the Object Navigator. The main goal here is to provide you with an overview of working in the environment.

8.3.1 My Objects

The My Objects view shows documents you've marked as favorites, last accessed, recently changed, and checked out. The general premise here is to help you get to documents that you're working or have worked on quickly. You no longer have to jot document numbers down on a piece of paper at your desk. You can count on the MY OBJECTS tab to keep track of the important documents.

You can personalize the MY OBJECTS tabs by changing the columns or adjusting which query (e.g., FAVORITE DOCUMENTS) is set as the default.

Additionally, a filter button is available so that you can filter the results to reduce the number of results shown or to find a specific document.

Favorites List and MyObjects

Figure 8.15 shows an example list of documents that a user has added to his favorites list via the additional functions in a document information record. This is included as a standard query of the MY OBJECTS view.

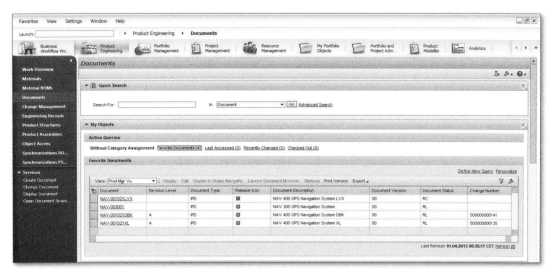

Figure 8.15 Document Added to the Favorites List as Displayed in the My Objects View

8.3.2 Simple Search

SAP offers a simple search and an advanced search for documents. In the simple search, you just input a key term that you're searching for, and all documents with some reference to the term as a document attribute or in an original file will be returned in the results screen, as shown in Figure 8.16. The technology behind this search is SAP Enterprise Search. Basically, an indexing job takes not only the contents of the original files but also the attributes (e.g., description, status, owner, etc.) of the document information record and creates a searchable index. This searchable index supports the simple search and advanced search capabilities.

Figure 8.16 shows a query entry for a simple search. Once executed, this will search across all indexed attributes to find related document information records.

8 | SAP PLM 7.02 DMS Web UI

Figure 8.16 Entering a Query for Simple Search

Figure 8.17 shows the resulting output of the search based on the input criteria.

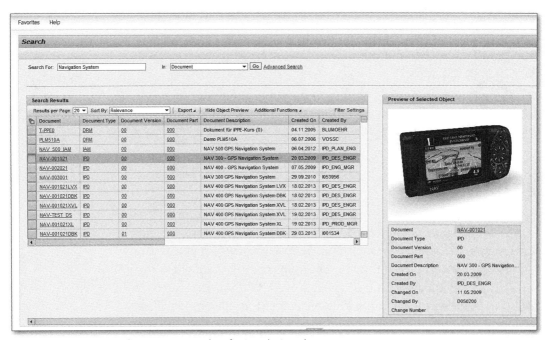

Figure 8.17 Results of a Simple Search

8.3.3 Advanced Search

The advanced search is very similar to what is offered in the SAP GUI Transaction CV04N (Find Document). You can search on a variety of attributes, including description, status, owner, and authorization group. You also can search on classification data, object links, and full text. As mentioned, it's very similar to what is offered via the SAP GUI Transaction CV04N. An additional feature that you might find useful is that you can save an existing query set and load it at later time. If you're using common search criteria often, it will save you the time of having to re-enter it each time.

Figure 8.18 shows the screen where you enter your search criteria when searching for documents. After the search is executed, the output is the same as a simple search.

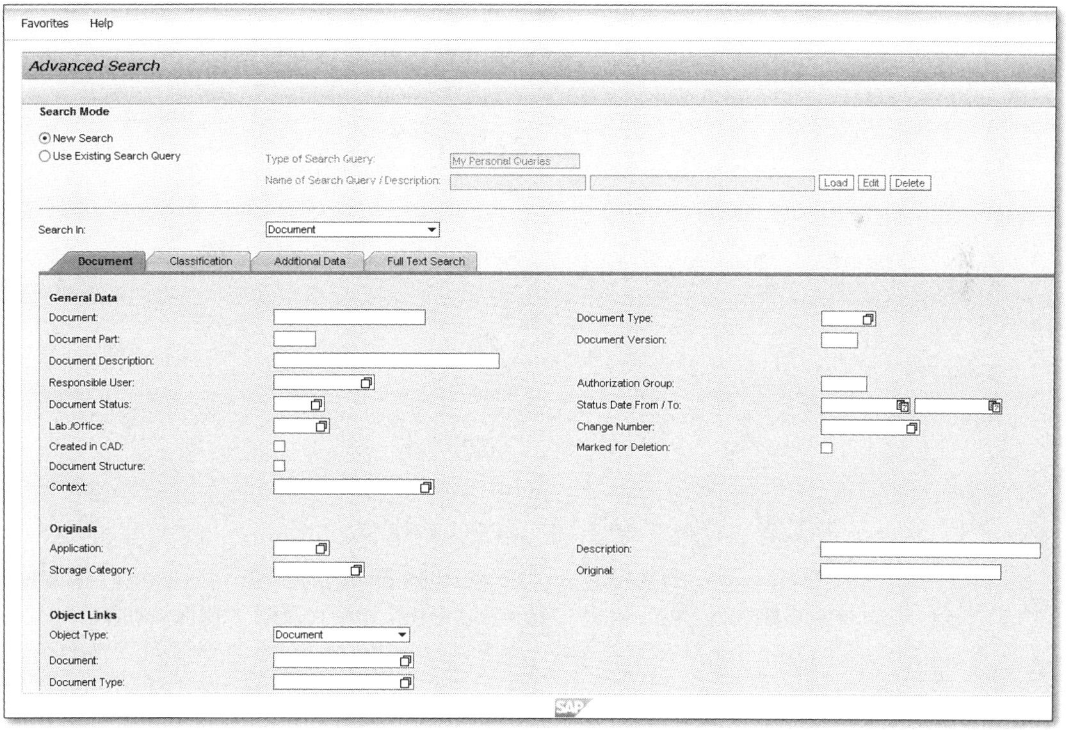

Figure 8.18 Advanced Search Screen for Entering Advanced Search Criteria

8.3.4 Side Panel

In the upper-right corner of the document information record, you'll find the SIDE PANEL link. The SIDE PANEL provides you with context-based reporting based on the specific document information record that is open. This is part of the larger set of functionality of the Business Context Viewer (BCV).

Figure 8.19 shows the SIDE PANEL for a specific document information record. In this case, the two query views shown are LATEST RELEASED VERSION FOR DOCUMENT and WORKFLOWS FOR DOCUMENT.

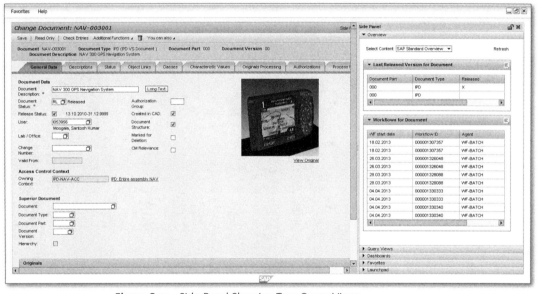

Figure 8.19 Side Panel Showing Two Query Views

8.3.5 "You Can Also" Functionality

As shown in Figure 8.20, the document information for the Web UI has a link called YOU CAN ALSO. Under this link, you'll find links to a variety of functions, including OPEN DOCUMENT BROWSER, DISPLAY ENGINEERING RECORD, and COPY DOCUMENT. Basically, the YOU CAN ALSO option list provides you a way to get to other areas of the system easily.

Additional Features of the SAP PLM 7.02 Web UI | 8.3

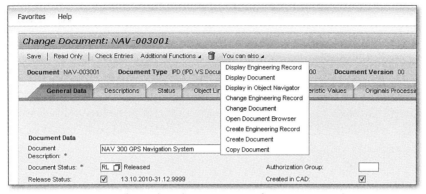

Figure 8.20 You Can Also Link in the Document Information Record

8.3.6 Object Navigator

As shown in Figure 8.21, the Object Navigator allows you to see a variety of information for a specific document information record, including object links, document structure, related change records, and where-used information. The Object Navigator helps you find key information related to document information records and reduces the effort involved in searching. You reach the Object Navigator via the YOU CAN ALSO link. Configuration options will be discussed later in the chapter.

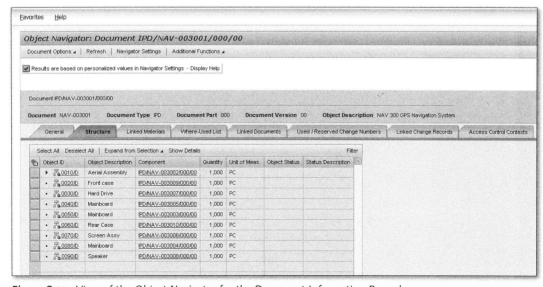

Figure 8.21 View of the Object Navigator for the Document Information Record

193

8.3.7 Personal Object Work List

The Personal Object Work List (POWL) allows you to create new queries simply and quickly that are available each time you log in to the system. For example, you might want to create a query that shows the last 25 documents you've created. Another example might be to show all documents that have a status of Released for a specific lab office. This feature and functionality offers you a way to keep track of documents that are important to you.

In Figure 8.22, the query activated for the POWL shows the latest released documents in the system.

Figure 8.22 Personal Object Work List Showing the Latest Released Files

Creating a POWL query

The steps for creating a new POWL query are as follows:

1. Select the DEFINE NEW QUERY link.

2. Select the object type. For this example, select POWL TYPE FOR DOCUMENT PERSONAL WORK LIST.

3. Select an existing query as a template. In this case, select DOCUMENTS PERSONAL WORK LIST. Click on the NEXT button.

4. In the next screen, enter your selection criteria. As an example, you want your worklist to display documents of a specific document type. To make this work, you select the document-specified type. After the selection criteria are complete, click on the NEXT button.

5. On the next secreen, you are prompted to enter a description for your new query and asked whether you want to activate it. Enter a name, and select that it should be active. This completes the process of creating a new query. You'll be returned to main PERSONAL OBJECT WORKLIST screen where your query will be displayed.

8.3.8 Document Browser

As shown in Figure 8.23, the DOCUMENT BROWSER resides in the main control center for the documents. The DOCUMENT BROWSER allows you to browse and work with folders that you've created via SAP Easy DMS or in the SAP GUI. From this screen, you can remove links, cut links, paste links, mark for deletion, and assign documents to a folder.

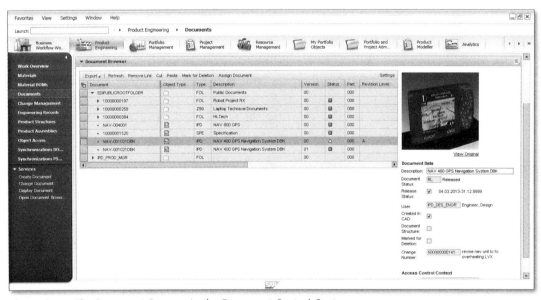

Figure 8.23 The Document Browser in the Document Control Center

8.3.9 Extended Document Browser

As shown in Figure 8.24, the extended Document Browser is much like the DOCUMENT BROWSER function displayed in the main control center. The major difference is that you are able to work directly with the document information records from the browser. As shown in Figure 8.25, you can select a document information record and directly update items such as the description, status, classification attributes, and object links. It provides you a method for working with many different document information records all within a single screen.

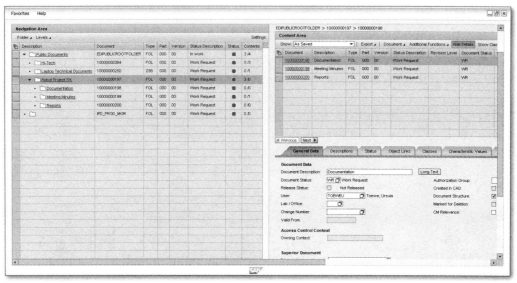

Figure 8.24 View of the Extended Document Browser

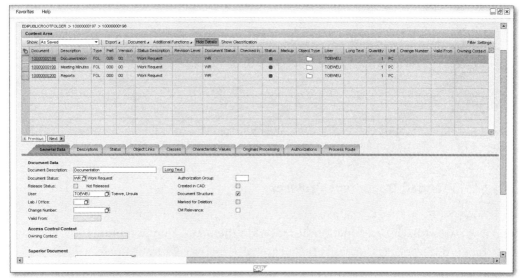

Figure 8.25 Working with a Specific Document in the Extended Document Browser

8.3.10 SAP PLM Web UI Inbox

As shown in Figure 8.26, the SAP PLM Web UI INBOX is where you'll see and execute the process route items you've created. The steps for processing a process route item are as follows:

Managing process routes with the Web UI

1. Select the process route item in the INBOX.
2. Click on the EXECUTE button. The document information record is opened. Complete any required actions, and close the document information record.
3. When ready, click on the COMPLETE button to complete the process route item.
4. You may also forward a process route to another user by clicking on the FORWARD button.

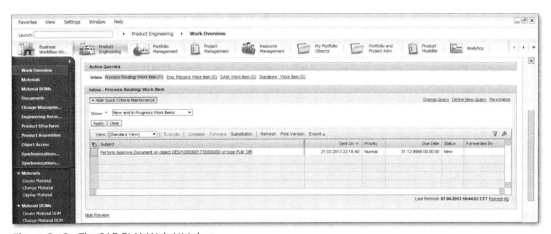

Figure 8.26 The SAP PLM Web UI Inbox

8.4 SAP PLM 7.02 DMS Web UI Additional Configuration Items

In this section, we'll discuss additional configuration and setup items related specifically to the SAP PLM 7.02 DMS Web UI. This includes items such as defining the correct workstation applications so that the SAP Visual Enterprise Viewer will be launched and enabling specific workflow objects to support the process route capability. This section isn't meant to be a definitive discussion of the SAP PLM 7.02 setup. Our focus here is on the items related to SAP DMS.

8.4.1 SAP IMG Configuration Items

To take advantage of the SAP PLM 7.02 DMS Web UI, you need to complete just a few configuration items. All of the configuration discussed in Chapter 4 is still relevant and serves as the foundation. The following configuration options are additional and focus on specific capabilities for the SAP PLM Web UI.

In the next sections, we'll cover each configuration item in some detail.

Define Document Types for Folder Creation

In this Customizing activity, you can define document types for creating document folders. This is specifically related to using the document structure function. As a standard, the document type FOL is defined as the standard document type when creating folders as shown in Figure 8.27, along with a view of the default configuration for folder types.

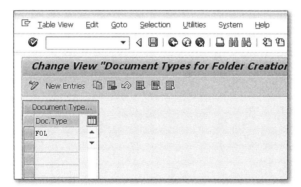

Figure 8.27 Configuration of Document Types for Folder Creation

As a prerequisite, the document type FOL (for "folder") should be configured via the standard document type configuration covered in Chapter 4. To make these configurations, follow the IMG path: SAP CUSTOMIZING IMPLEMENTATION GUIDE • LOGISTICS GENERAL • PRODUCT LIFECYCLE MANAGEMENT (PLM) • PLM WEB USER INTERFACE • OBJECTS IN PLM WEB

UI • DOCUMENT IN PLM WEB UI • DEFINE DOCUMENT TYPES FOR FOLDER CREATION.

Define Search Sequence for Viewable File

In this Customizing activity, you define the search sequence for choosing files from SAP objects—for example, BOM, material, and document—to be displayed as a thumbnail or in the viewer. You can link a file from an SAP object to documents and either display them as thumbnails or in the viewer. Figure 8.28 shows an example configuration.

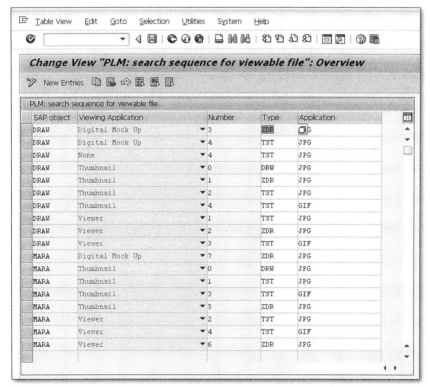

Figure 8.28 Example Configuration for Defining the Search Sequence for Viewable Files

The configuration options are found via the following IMG path: SAP CUSTOMIZING IMPLEMENTATION GUIDE • LOGISTICS GENERAL • PRODUCT LIFECYCLE MANAGEMENT (PLM) • PLM WEB USER INTERFACE • OBJECTS IN

PLM W‌eb UI • Document in PLM W‌eb UI • Define Search Sequence for Viewable File. The following options are available for this configuration:

- In the SAP object field, enter the SAP object that you want to display as thumbnails or in the viewer.
- In the Viewing Application field, choose whether the file is displayed as a thumbnail or in the viewer.
- In the Number field, enter a sequence number that the system uses when searching for files.
- In the Type field, enter the document type to select the thumbnail from.
- In the Application field, enter the workstation application to select.

Define Workstation Application

Configuring workstation application specific to PLM 7.02 DMS Web UI

This configuration item has been discussed in Chapter 4 and deals with Customizing settings you have to make to process an original file. The difference here is that the SAP PLM 7.02 DMS Web UI is using the Visual Enterprise Viewer as the new integrated viewer, so you'll want to make adjustments in the configuration to support this new viewer. This SAP Visual Enterprise Viewer supports formats such as JPG, GIF, TIF, DWF, and BMP from a 2D perspective. Additionally, it supports a whole variety of 3D formats such as RH, 3DS, and VRML. All in all, the SAP Visual Enterprise Viewer supports well over 50 different formats and is continuously updated as new requirements appear.

The following SAP page has an updated listing of currently supported file formats: *http://help.sap.com/saphelp_ve71/helpdata/EN/be/df68d83eae-430f892ed29522bf6744/content.htm*.

For example, the SAP Visual Enterprise Viewer supports viewing GIF files, and you want to use the internal viewer to view GIF files in the SAP DMS Web UI. In the configuration for the workstation application, you should enter "%VIEWER-CONTROL%%SAPPROVIS%" in the application configuration for JPG (go to the following IMG path: SAP Customizing Implementation Guide • Logistics General • Product Lifecycle Management (PLM) • Document Management • General

Data • Define Workstation Application). The example configuration is shown in Figure 8.29.

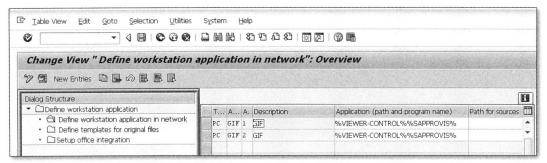

Figure 8.29 Example Configuration of the Workstation Application GIF to Call the SAP Visual Enterprise Viewer

Icon for Release Status

You can activate the release status icon in SAP PLM Web UI Document. This icon is displayed when the document information reaches a Released status, as defined by the individual status network. To make this configure, go to the following IMG path: SAP Customizing Implementation Guide • Logistics General • Product Lifecycle Management (PLM) • PLM Web User Interface • Objects in PLM Web UI • Document in PLM Web UI • Icon for Release Status. The configuration setting is shown in Figure 8.30.

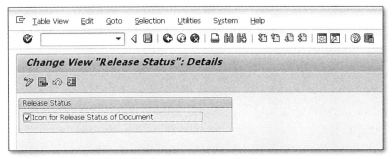

Figure 8.30 Activation of Release Status Icon for Documents

Updating the "You Can Also" via Transaction LPD_CUST

The contents of the YOU CAN ALSO link are controlled via SAP Transaction LPD_CUST. In this transaction, you add, change, and delete items from the list. Therefore, it's easy to add calls to additional transactions or programs. In Figure 8.31, you see the contents of the current YOU CAN ALSO link for the document information record. From here, you can start your updates.

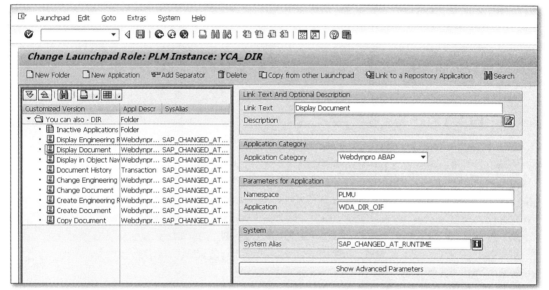

Figure 8.31 The You Can Also Link Settings for the SAP PLM Web UI Document Information Record

Setup Viewer Application

DMU viewing

As shown in Figure 8.32, you can define the entries that are relevant for digital mockup viewing (DMU viewing), such as the DMU EXPLOSION setting and the geometric data (GEO. DATA) setting, as well as the redlining identifier. The entries made here are dependent on the application where the viewer is used, so the application building block ID (ABB ID) must be maintained accordingly. This means that for different ABB IDs, different settings can be made. If no ABB ID is maintained for an application, the default entry is used. To access the configuration, go to the following IMG path: SAP CUSTOMIZING IMPLEMENTATION GUIDE • LOGISTICS GENERAL •

PRODUCT LIFECYCLE MANAGEMENT (PLM) • PLM WEB USER INTERFACE • PLM WEB APPLICATIONS • VIEWER • DEFINE VIEWER APPLICATION.

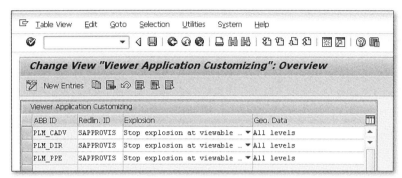

Figure 8.32 Example Viewer Application Configuration

Object Navigator

In this Customizing activity, you make settings for the object types that you can display on the OBJECT NAVIGATOR screen, as well as which views (which appear as tab pages on the UI) you can see for each central object type (see Figure 8.33). This includes the document information record and how the relations between objects in these views are displayed.

For the document information record type, you can control the following:

- Views that are displayed
- View layout for each view displayed
- Relations between different object types
- Specific view variants
- Relations you want to display or hide in a particular view variant
- Rankings for each view variant
- Columns to be displayed for each object type
- Order of columns to be displayed for each object type
- Which parameters aren't considered for personalization

The configuration in this area is very powerful and flexible. The goal here is to be able to tailor and present only the most important information to users. To make these configurations, go to the following IMG path: SAP

8 | SAP PLM 7.02 DMS Web UI

Customizing Implementation Guide • Logistics General • Product Lifecycle Management (PLM) • PLM Web User Interface • PLM Web Applications • Setting for Object Navigator • Make Settings for Object Navigator.

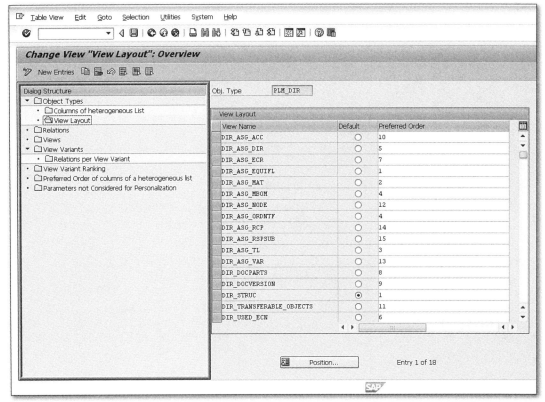

Figure 8.33 Sample Object Navigator View Layout for the Document Information Record

Process Routes

To use process routes, you need to have the basic system settings for workflow completed. This is done via the automatic workflow Customizing Transaction SWU3. After the general workflow is complete, you should follow these general steps to fully enable the process route:

1. Activate event linkage for the main workflow WS100012. This is maintained via Transaction PFTC_DIS. Choose the task type workflow template, enter the number "100012", and display the workflow.

    Steps to enable a process route

2. Open the TRIGGERING EVENTS tab page, and activate the event by clicking on the symbol in the first column.

3. Maintain possible processors for the task TS100010. You also maintain this in Transaction PFTC_DIS. Choose the task type STANDARD TASK, enter the number "100010", and display the task.

4. Choose ADDITIONAL DATA • PROCESSOR ASSIGNMENT • MAINTAIN. If you don't want to make any restrictions, choose the ATTRIBUTES button, and select General Task.

5. Refresh the organizational environment in Transaction SWUS. Enter the workflow "WS100012", and choose ENVIRONMENT • REFRESH ORGANIZATIONAL ENVIRONMENT.

6. When complete, you'll be able to use the process route capabilities in the system.

White List Setup

To store or display original files in the SAP DMS Web UI, you need to set up a white list. This is a requirement specific to the Web UI. The white list controls the following options when working with original files associated with a document information record:

White list controls

- Only certain listed file extensions (e.g., PDF, XLS, DOC) are allowed to be processed. A sample configuration of this is shown in Figure 8.34.

- Only authorized executable programs on the client PC are triggered (e.g., *C:\Program Files (x86)\Adobe\Reader 11.0\Reader\AcroRd32.exe*).

- Data can only be stored in authorized directories (e.g., *c:\temp\download*).

- Data can only be read from authorized directories (e.g., *c:\temp\upload*).

- Content servers are accessible for upload/download (e.g., *http://abc.com:1090*).

You'll need to complete the setup of the white list before you can start working with files in the SAP DMS Web UI. Follow these steps:

1. Execrure Transaction WDR_ACF_WLIST (Create Security List).
2. On the initial screen, click on the change pencil icon.
3. Create a new entry called "DEFAULT".
4. For the "DEFAULT" entry, select the WHITE LIST FOR FILE EXTENSIONS, APPLIKATION, and DOWNLOAD, AND UPLOAD options.
5. Save the new entry.
6. Return to the initial screen of the transaction, and click on the INSTALL CERTIFICATE toolbar button. This installs a certificate on your local machine and allows you to work with files you've defined.

> **Note**
> If a certificate doesn't exist, use Transaction WDR_ACF_GEN_CERT to generate the certificate.

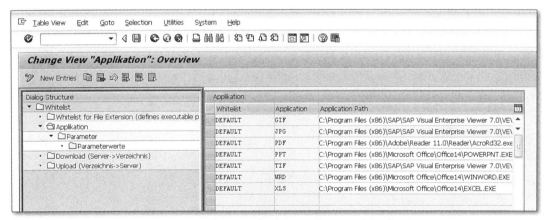

Figure 8.34 Sample View of White List Setup and Applications

White list capabilities and setup are quickly changing. With technology and security requirements changing, the functionality and configuration of the white list also changes. To be sure you are up to date, review the latest SAP Help and SAP notes to confirm the latest process.

8.5 Summary

In this chapter, we've provided a introduction to the SAP PLM 7.02 Web UI with a focus on SAP DMS functions. We went through a simple exercise of creating a new document information record in the new Web UI and discussed some of the differences between what you'll find in the Web UI and the backend SAP DMS system. Beyond SAP DMS, we took a look at the basic capabilities you'll find in the SAP PLM 7.02 Web UI, including Personal Object Work Lists, Inbox capabilities, searching, and the Document Browser. The goal here was to provide you with knowledge of the available tools and what is possible when working with the new environment. Finally, we took a look at configuration items related to SAP PLM 7.02 Web UI with a focus on SAP DMS functions. This included setting up the white list, viewer application, and Object Navigator configuration. You should now have a good idea of the SAP PLM 7.02 Web UI capabilities and configuration in relation to SAP DMS.

In the next chapter we'll discuss integrating CAD tools into the SAP system.

This chapter takes a closer look at how you can use SAP-provided integration interfaces to store and manage CAD data in SAP DMS.

9   Integrating a CAD System to SAP DMS

In this chapter, you'll learn about integrating CAD systems into SAP DMS. First, you'll learn which interfaces are available to get an idea whether it's possible to integrate a specific CAD system into SAP DMS. You'll then learn about the capabilities and benefits of integrating a CAD system to SAP DMS. Next, we'll introduce you to the SAP CAD Desktop and walk through a simple sample CAD integration scenario.

Note that this chapter is meant to be an introduction to a broad topic; in fact, there could easily be a separate chapter for explaining how to work with each CAD interface. This is because each CAD package is unique and has its own set of rules on how it functions. Providing this detailed information is, however, beyond the scope of this book. Therefore, you should select the CAD interface you intend to use and simply start working with it. You can also gather good information from the partners who work directly with SAP to develop the interfaces. They have a wealth of knowledge and provide excellent support during implementation.

9.1   Available SAP CAD Integration Interfaces

Table 9.1 lists the CAD systems that have a direct integration interface to SAP DMS. You can purchase interfaces directly from SAP. Each CAD interface is created jointly between SAP and a development partner who specializes in the respective CAD tool.

CAD Interface	Development Partners
AutoCAD	Cideon
AutoDesk Inventor	Cideon
CATIA V4	Cenit
CATIA V5	Cenit
I-deas	Tesis
ME10	DSC
Medusa	DSC
Microstation	Cideon
Pro/Engineer	.riess
Solid Edge	Cideon
SolidWorks	Cideon
Unigraphics	DSC

Table 9.1 CAD Interfaces Available with Development Partners

9.2 Capabilities and Benefits of CAD Interfaces

Because each CAD tool is unique, there will be different benefits and capabilities to each interface. However, certain standard capabilities and benefits exist because the CAD integration interfaces have been designed to provide a similar set of capabilities.

9.2.1 Capabilities

Typically, each CAD integration interface will provide the following capabilities:

- Secure storage of CAD data
- Execution of relevant SAP DMS transactions that support the management of CAD data, directly from the CAD tool
- Maintenance of the structure and relationships when storing or changing the CAD data, if you're using a CAD tool (e.g., CATIA V5) that maintains a structure and relationship between models

- Use of SAP Engineering Change Management tools on stored CAD data
- Creating, changing, and displaying supporting master data objects such as material masters and BOMs
- Generation of a neutral file of the stored CAD data to allow viewing of data by users who don't have a CAD application

9.2.2 Benefits

Along with the just mentioned capabilities, you can expect the following benefits when using one of the CAD integration interfaces:

- CAD data is secure, and updates are controlled.
- You can use SAP Engineering Change Management tools to control data creation and updates. You can also create a more formal process that involves workflow and approvals for managing the lifecycle of the data.
- Data is visible to others who may need access for decision making.
- Storage of CAD data can be the initiation point for the creation of material masters and BOMs.
- After CAD data is stored, additional processes can be triggered, such as an approval or review workflow.
- Neutral files can be generated for viewing by users who don't have access to the CAD application.
- You move away from managing files to actually managing the process for creation and change of CAD data.

9.3 SAP CAD Desktop

As shown in Figure 9.1, the CAD Desktop (Transaction: CDESK) is the tool provided by SAP for managing CAD data in SAP DMS after it's transferred from the CAD application. It lets you manage single documents and document structures for CAD applications that use an assembly type structure. Some of its basic functions include the following:

9 | Integrating a CAD System to SAP DMS

CAD Desktop functions
- Creating a document information record for a model or drawing being stored
- Changing the status of a document information record
- Checking in and checking out original files
- Creating a material master for a given document information record
- Creating a BOM based on the document structure and related materials
- Changing data with relation to an engineering change master

As mentioned, these are the basic functions of the CAD Desktop. It has many other capabilities, including synchronizing attributes between the document information record and the title block of the drawing, which are best understood and demonstrated by using one of the CAD integration interfaces.

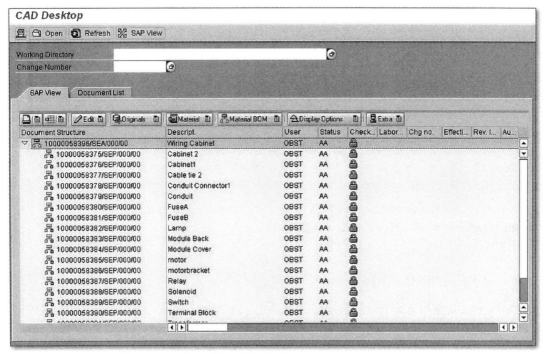

Figure 9.1 View of the CAD Desktop

From a technical standpoint, communication between the CAD application and the CAD Desktop is accomplished through remote function calls (RFCs). This allows transfer or creation of data in SAP DMS directly from the CAD application. You don't necessarily need to open the SAP GUI to execute functions. You can work comfortably in your CAD application.

In the next section, we'll discuss an example of how the CAD integration can be used.

9.4 Example CAD Integration Scenario

To give you an idea of the steps a user needs to take when working with one of the SAP CAD integration interfaces, consider the following example.

> **Example**
>
> You own a company that designs bicycles. All new bicycles start with an initial design in your CAD application. Data that is generated in your CAD application needs to be stored in SAP DMS for a variety of reasons, including secure storage and the ability to share the data with others in remote offices.
>
> To create and store the CAD data into SAP DMS for this example, you follow these steps:.
>
> 1. **Create the CAD data representing the new bicycle design.** In your CAD application, create the CAD data, such as models and drawings.
>
> 2. **From the CAD application, execute the menu item to store CAD data in SAP DMS.** At a certain maturity level, you'll store the generated CAD data back into SAP DMS. Through a menu item in the CAD application, transfer the CAD data from the CAD application to the SAP CAD Desktop.
>
> 3. **Create document information records.** For each CAD model or drawing, create a corresponding document information record. From the CAD Desktop, you can select the newly transferred CAD data and create the document information records in bulk. Fill in all required attributes.
>
> 4. **Create material masters.** For each part of the bicycle assembly, create a material master. The material master created here will be the starting definition for each part. This will be extended at a later point to include information such as how to manufacture, procure, or sell the part.
>
> 5. **Create a BOM.** For the assembly, create a BOM. This is the parts list or structure of what parts go into building the bicycle. It's made from the material masters that were created in the previous step.

> 6. **Check in the CAD data.** Check in the CAD data to move it from your local storage to the SAP DMS content server. This will make it possible for you to share the data with others.
> 7. **Exit the SAP CAD Desktop.** Exit the SAP CAD Desktop to return to your CAD application.
> 8. **The process is complete, so close the CAD application.** You can later retrieve the CAD data that was stored into SAP DMS and continue making modifications.

9.5 CAD Data Migration

When implementing one of the CAD interfaces, you should consider how you'll handle data migration of existing CAD data into SAP DMS. This can be a simple process or a very complex one. As an example of a simple data migration, let's say that you're interfacing AutoCAD to SAP DMS, and you want to migrate all of your legacy AutoCAD files into SAP DMS. For AutoCAD, there are no relationships between each file. Therefore, it's a fairly simple process to create a new document information record for each file and add the AutoCAD file as an original file. As an example of a complex data-migration process, let's say that you're working with a CAD tool such as CATIA V5 or UG NX and using assembly structures. This means that you'll have to carefully load the CAD data into SAP DMS so that relationships between files are maintained, and the assembly structure remains intact. This can be done on a one-by-one basis, or with tools that are developed by some of the CAD partners mentioned previously in Table 9.1.

9.6 SAP Visual Enterprise Tools and CAD Data

When to use the Visual Experience Viewer versus the Visual Enterprise Author

After CAD data is managed with SAP DMS, you'll be able to take advantage of SAP's Visual Enterprise tools, including the Visual Enterprise Generator, Viewer, and Author. Definitions of these tools are provided in Table 9.2. These tools are additional to what is delivered as part of SAP DMS. On a system-defined trigger (e.g., a status change of the document information record), you can trigger the SAP Visual Enterprise Generator to create lightweight versions of the stored 3D CAD data for consumption throughout the organization. Traditionally, only those who had licenses to the CAD software packages could gain access to this data. Once available, you can use the SAP Visual Enterprise Viewer for viewing the lightweight files and use the SAP Visual Enterprise Author for manipulating the CAD data into a variety of outputs, including service and marketing material.

Tool	Description
SAP Visual Enterprise Generator	A graphical processing client-server application that allows you to automate the processing of CAD and other 2D and 3D graphics to support specific work processes in engineering, manufacturing, and maintenance. You can create enterprise solutions that translate nearly any 3D CAD file into a lightweight format for downstream use, enabling nontechnical users to search, access, manipulate, and integrate complex graphical data into any business or office application across your organization.
SAP Visual Enterprise Author	A desktop application used to create 3D animations and render rich visual content into common desktop documents, file formats, and business applications for secure downstream use. You can manage 2D, 3D, animation, video, and audio assets, with support for opening and importing all supported CAD file formats.
SAP Visual Enterprise Viewer	Supports viewing of lightweight 3D models and other formats (e.g., JPG) generated from SAP Visual Enterprise Generator.

Table 9.2 Definition of SAP Visual Enterprise Tools

9.7 Summary

This chapter provided a brief introduction to the topic of integrating a CAD system into SAP DMS. We covered the available SAP CAD integration interfaces and reviewed some of the capabilities and benefits of integrating your CAD system to SAP DMS. We also took a quick look at the SAP CAD Desktop and at a typical CAD integration scenario. Additionally, we discussed different SAP Visual Enterprise tools, along with the key capabilities which they offer. In the next chapter, we'll cover the creation of a simple document approval process using SAP Workflow.

This chapter provides instructions on how to set up a simple approval process using SAP Workflow based on a document status change.

10 Simple Document Approval Process using SAP Workflow

An approval process for a document information record can be as simple or complex as needed. In this chapter, we'll look at the fundamental steps and tools to create a basic document approval process using SAP Workflow. When you understand these methods, you can expand the process to include more intricate working models.

First, we'll look at the workflow scenario, the required elements of configuration, how to create a workflow definition, and finally how to test it.

10.1 The Workflow Scenario

For our scenario, a document information record being set to the status of Review initiates a workflow notification that is sent to a reviewer. Within the workflow notification is a link to the document information record, allowing the reviewer instant access to the data. If it's approved, the reviewer sets the status of the document information record to "Released." If not approved, the reviewer sets the status back to "In Work." A workflow notification is sent to the initiator of the workflow with the results of the review.

10.2 Required SAP DMS and Workflow Configuration

Some SAP DMS configuration is required before proceeding with workflow setup. The requirements are as follows:

- Create a new document type ZSA (Simple Approval Demo) with a status network of In Work, Review, and Released.

> **Note**
> Instead of creating a new document type from scratch, you can copy one of the standard document types that are delivered with the SAP system, such as DRW. After the copy, you'll need to modify the status network.

- Allow users to change the status of the document information record from "In Work" to "Review," "Review" to "In Work," and "Review" to "Released."

After you've completed the required configuration, you can move on to the SAP Workflow system. The SAP Workflow system must be configured for this example to work. Because this guide doesn't focus on SAP Workflow, the steps for configuration aren't covered here. To check whether basic SAP Workflow settings are complete, execute Transaction SWU3 (Automatic Workflow Customizing). If settings aren't complete, refer to SAP Help for the steps to complete them.

10.3 Creating the Workflow Definition

This section covers the steps to create the workflow definition. The workflow definition encompasses how the workflow will be triggered and what steps or tasks will happen during the workflow.

10.3.1 Execute Transaction PFTC (Task: Maintain)

Transaction PFTC is used to define the workflow you're building. Because this will be a multi-step workflow definition, select task type WORKFLOW TEMPLATE, and click on the CREATE button, as shown in Figure 10.1. This is the first step in creating a workflow definition.

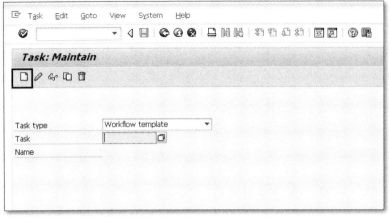

Figure 10.1 Task Maintain Entry Screen

10.3.2 Enter Information on the Basic Data Tab of the Workflow Definition

The next step in creating a workflow definition is to fill in the information on the BASIC DATA tab. This information is important because it specifies how you'll search for the workflow definition and identify that it's a release workflow definition. The field values you'll enter on the BASIC DATA tab are displayed in Table 10.1. The fields, as illustrated in Figure 10.2, are straightforward. The field ABBR. is a short abbreviation given to the workflow definition. The field NAME provides a short description for the workflow definition. The field RELEASE STATUS identifies what state the workflow definition is in.

Field	Value
ABBR.	"ZSIMAPPR"
NAME	"Simple Document Approval Process"
RELEASED STATUS	RELEASED

Table 10.1 Basic Data Tab Field Values

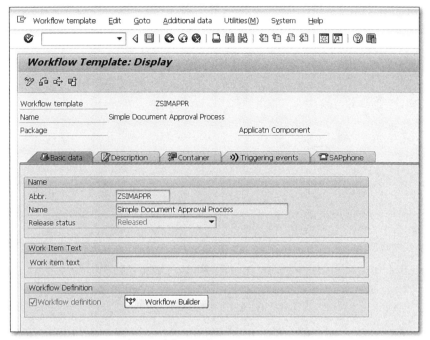

Figure 10.2 Basic Data for Workflow Definition

10.3.3 Create New Container Element

After you've completed the BASIC DATA tab, the next step is to create a new container element. The *container element* is like a vessel and specifies how data is passed from the triggering event to the workflow and the task. For this example, we're creating a container element for the document information record. When the workflow is triggered by changing the status of the document information record, all of the information about the document information record (e.g., description, owner, status, etc.) will be passed from the event and put into the container element. Therefore, you can work with this data to make decisions in the workflow, such as whether the workflow should be triggered or who should review it.

To create a new container element, you must first select the CONTAINER tab. Define a new container element, and call it "Document." To do this, click on the toolbar button on the far left of the tab, called CREATE ELEMENT. Enter data as shown in Figure 10.3 and Figure 10.4. This includes providing a name, short description, and object type, and also setting the properties of import/export for the new container element. This information is entered on the D.TYPE tab and the PROPERTIES tab.

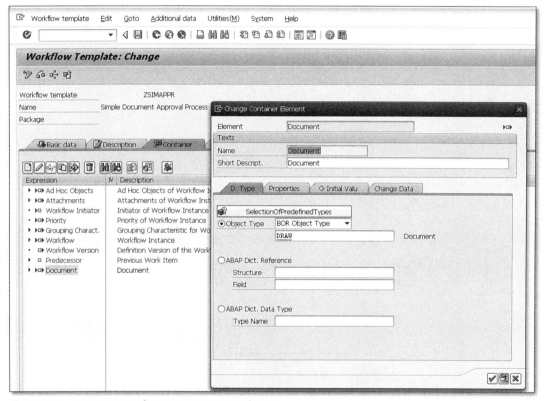

Figure 10.3 Basic Settings for a New Container Element

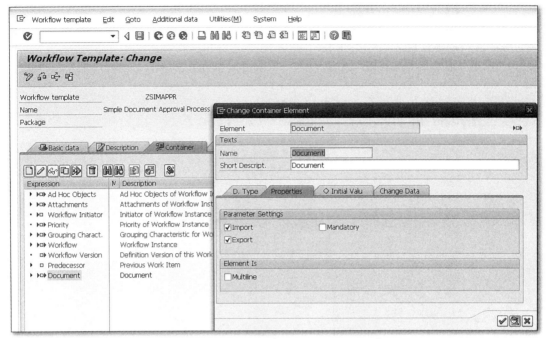

Figure 10.4 Property Settings for a New Container Element

10.3.4 Save the Workflow Definition

After clicking on the SAVE icon, a screen labeled CREATE OBJECT DIRECTORY ENTRY appears. Click on the LOCAL OBJECT button. This assigns the new workflow to package $TMP, and a new internal number is generated for the workflow definition, as shown in Figure 10.5.

Figure 10.5 Workflow Template Number Assigned and Associated to Package $TMP

10.3.5 Add Triggering Event

Select the TRIGGERING EVENTS tab, which is where you'll identify how the workflow will start. The workflow you're defining will start when a document information record is changed in some way. We'll further refine the starting event at a later point in the process so that the workflow starts for a defined document type and status change.

Starting a workflow with triggering events

As shown in Figure 10.6, select an OBJECT CATEGORY of BOR OBJECT TYPE, an OBJECT TYPE of DRAW, and an EVENT of CHANGED. After entering values, click on the far-left button in the event creator column to activate the event. This button is currently green, to identify that the triggering event is activated and the workflow will start when this event is raised in the system.

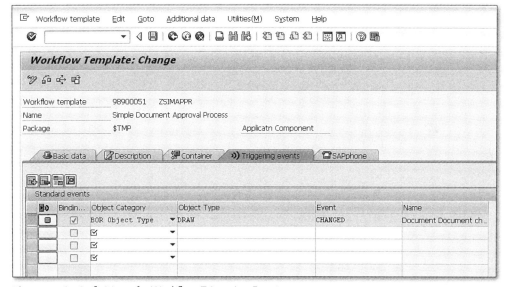

Figure 10.6 Definition of a Workflow Triggering Event

10.3.6 Start the Workflow Builder

The Workflow Builder is where you'll define the flow or what tasks will be executed during the workflow. You'll also define additional start conditions, which is the first step. To start the Workflow Builder, click on the WORKFLOW BUILDER button near the bottom of the screen in the workflow definition section.

10.3.7 Set the Additional Start Conditions

Setting additional start conditions will specify that the workflow will only start for a certain document type and status. This is important because a general triggering event was set when the workflow definition was created. This needs to be refined so that it isn't triggered every time a document is changed.

To set the additional start conditions, click on the BASIC DATA icon in the WORKFLOW BUILDER toolbar. Next, select the START EVENTS tab, and click on the START CONDITION button, as shown in Figure 10.7.

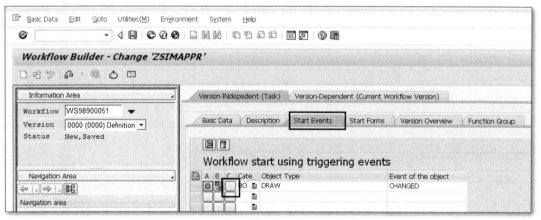

Figure 10.7 The Start Events Tab

In the condition builder, set the condition DOCUMENT TYPE equal to "ZSA" and DOCUMENT STATUS equal to "IR" as shown in Figure 10.8. This workflow will now start only for document type ZSA and status RV.

Transport requests

You can use the check function in the condition builder to make sure your condition is set correctly. If it's correct, click on the green checkmark button to return to the previous screen. If required, input a transport request. A transport request tracks the changes you're making. Use the back button to return to the main WORKFLOW BUILDER screen.

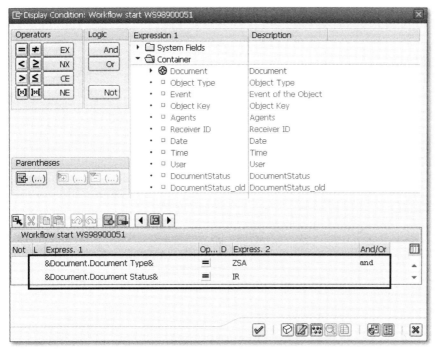

Figure 10.8 The Condition Builder with Conditions Entered

10.3.8 Add Tasks to the Workflow

The next step is adding tasks to the workflow. As shown in Figure 10.9, you can create a new activity by right-clicking on the undefined activity in the main WORKFLOW BUILDER screen and selecting CREATE. In the STEP SELECTION screen, select ACTIVITY.

As shown in Figure 10.10, on the ACTIVITY definition screen, you can select TASK TS000007842 and the function COPY AND EDIT TASK.

10 | Simple Document Approval Process using SAP Workflow

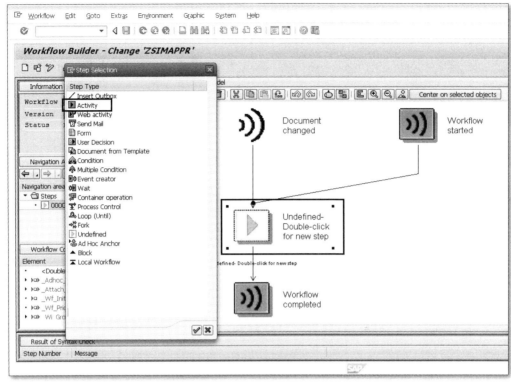

Figure 10.9 Selecting an Undefined Activity and Calling the Step Selection Screen

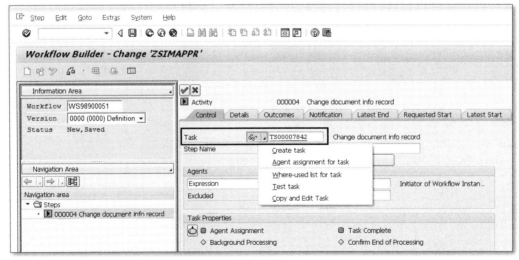

Figure 10.10 The Activity Definition Screen

The STANDARD TASK SCREEN is for container elements and binding. Click on the green checkmark button to accept the system recommendations.

Another screen appears with the heading COPY TASK. In the field ABBR., add a "Z" to the front of DRAW CHANGE. Click on the COPY TASK button.

On the CREATE OBJECT DIRECTORY entry screen, click on the LOCAL OBJECT button. This places the new task into the development package $TMP and takes you to the main screen for defining the task.

In the work item text, replace the words "was changed" with "Ready for Review." Don't change anything else.

On the TERMINATING EVENTS tab, configure the setting so that the workflow item will terminate or complete when the document is changed. Set ELEMENT equal to "_WI_OBJECT_ID" and EVENT equal to "CHANGED", as shown in Figure 10.11.

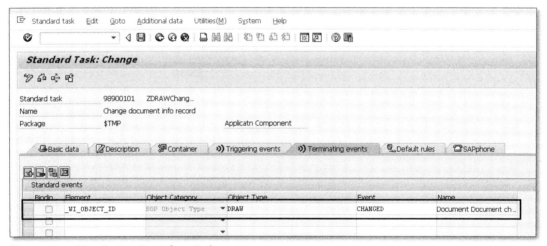

Figure 10.11 Terminating Event for a Task

The new task must be set to be a general task. A *general task* can be executed by anyone in the system. To set the general task, follow the menu path ADDITIONAL DATA • AGENT ASSIGNMENT • MAINTAIN.

General tasks

As shown in Figure 10.12, select the task, and click on the ATTRIBUTES button. Select GENERAL TASK, and click on the TRANSFER button. Use the BACK button to get back to the main task definition screen. The task can now be executed by everyone in the system. It's also possible to restrict execution of the task to a group of users.

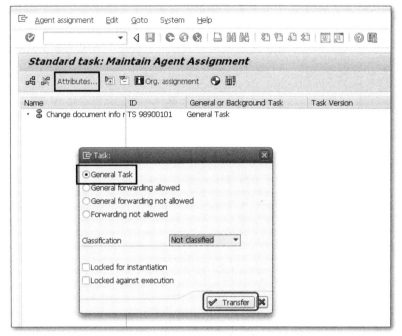

Figure 10.12 Setting a New Task as a General Task

Save the task, and use the green arrow button to return to the ACTIVITY definition screen. The new task number will be populated. In this case, the new task number is TS98900101, as shown in Figure 10.13.

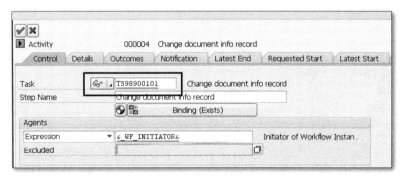

Figure 10.13 The New Task Number Populated

Set the agent to execute the workflow task to the initiator of the workflow so that the user who triggers the workflow will receive the notification to review the document. This is a simple scenario and can be configured to be much more complex, such as selecting an agent based on the document type and status.

In the AGENTS area, set the expression to &_WF_INITIATOR&. Click on the green checkmark to transfer the task to the workflow definition. Your workflow definition should now look like the one shown in Figure 10.14.

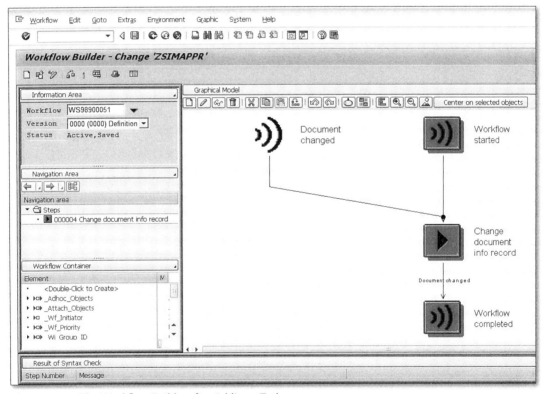

Figure 10.14 The Workflow Builder after Adding a Task

Add another task to the workflow so that the initiator of the workflow is notified when the review process is complete.

Right-click on the element DOCUMENT CHANGED in the WORKFLOW BUILDER, and select CREATE. From the STEP SELECTION menu, select SEND

MAIL. As mentioned previously, an email will be sent after the review is complete.

Send Mail tasks

For the SEND MAIL task definition, on the MAIL tab, enter a RECIPIENT TYPE of organizational object with an EXPRESSION of &_WF_INITIATOR&. This way, the workflow initiator will receive notification that the review has been completed. In the SUBJECT field, enter "Review Document &DOCUMENT.DOCUMENTNUMBER& Complete". This is the subject line of the notification the reviewer will receive. In the lower text area, enter the message you want to send. All of this information is shown in Figure 10.15.

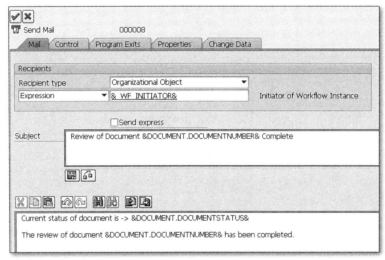

Figure 10.15 The Send Mail Task Definition

To insert dynamic expressions, use the INSERT EXPRESSIONS button in the SUBJECT area.

After entering the information, use the green arrow button to return to the WORKFLOW BUILDER. You'll be asked to provide a task abbreviation and name. Enter the information of your choice. Click on the green checkmark button. On the screen that displays, save the object as a local object. The SEND MAIL task will be transferred to your workflow definition.

10.3.9 Activate the Workflow

Now that you've completed the workflow definition, the last step is activating the workflow. As shown in Figure 10.16, click on the ACTIVATE button in the main toolbar to save and activate the workflow in the system.

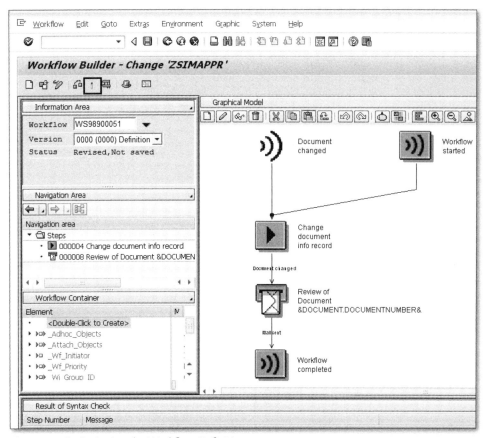

Figure 10.16 Activating the Workflow Definition

10.4 Execute and Test the Workflow

In the system, execute the following steps to test the workflow you built in the previous steps:

1. Execute Transaction CV01N to create a new document information record. On the first screen, enter document type "ZSA", and press ⏎Enter.

2. On the next screen, in the DOCUMENT DATA area, enter a short description in the DESCRIPTION field, and save the change.

3. Open the new document information record in change mode and set the status to REVIEW.

4. Open your SAP Business Workplace using Transaction SBWP. In the INBOX, locate and select the WORKFLOW 1 folder. As shown in Figure 10.17, locate the workflow notification for the document information record that was set to a status of REVIEW. Double-click on the workflow notification to access the document information record.

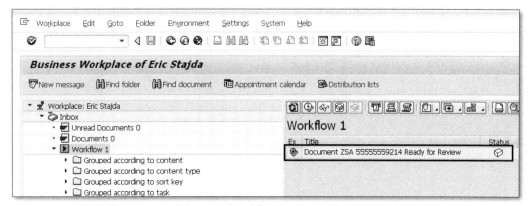

Figure 10.17 Inbox with Workflow Item to Review Document

5. Set the status on the document information record to RELEASED, and save the change.

6. Select the INBOX folder, and update it using the UPDATE icon in the upper-left corner of the inbox toolbar. As shown in Figure 10.18, an email notification appears stating that the document review has been completed. Double-click on the email notification. You'll see that the review has been completed, along with the current status of the document.

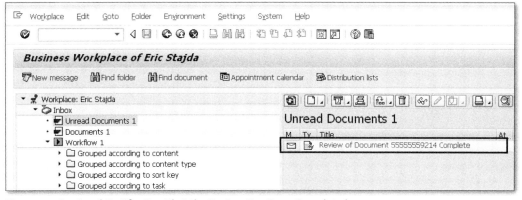

Figure 10.18 Email Notification That the Review Has Been Completed

10.5 Summary

In this chapter, we provided you with a simple demonstration of the tools and methods for SAP Workflow. You should now understand triggering events and how to build a workflow definition. It's also possible to create much more complex scenarios, such as the following:

- Creating an ad hoc approval process where the approvers are assigned at triggering.
- Instead of triggering the workflow by status change, starting the workflow manually through generic object services
- Creating a serial approval process, where additional approvers are sent notification after one approves
- Triggering a workflow based on a redline or markup being added

In the next chapter, we'll take a look at the different BAdIs and user exits available to further customize SAP DMS.

This chapter provides definitions, methods, and examples for SAP DMS BAdIs and user exits, which can be used to expand the standard out-of-the-box SAP DMS functionality.

11 SAP DMS BAdIs and User Exits

SAP has an excellent out-of-the-box DMS that can be configured to meet most business requirements. However, in some situations, additional business rules must be implemented that aren't supported through IMG configuration. In these cases, SAP provides you with a number of Business Add-Ins (BAdIs) and user exits that help you expand the standard functionality of SAP DMS. Throughout this chapter, we'll review the different BAdIs and explain when and why you should use them.

11.1 About SAP BAdIs and User Exits

BAdIs and user exits differ in a number of ways. In terms of age, BAdIs are the newer technology based on ABAP Objects; however, the user exits in the system remain available from earlier releases. One major difference between a BAdI and a user exit is that you can implement a BAdI multiple times. This isn't possible with a user exit because you have only one instance and location to include additional code. SAP also guarantees upward compatibility of BAdI interfaces. This lowers the risk of rework when upgrading to a new release of SAP.

To review a BAdI, use Transaction SE18 (Business Add-Ins). Reviewing the available methods, as shown in Figure 11.1, will give you an excellent idea of what is possible. For example, the BAdI listed (DOCUMENT_MAIN01) has methods for adding additional code before save (BEFORE_SAVE) of the document information and also after save (AFTER_SAVE).

Reviewing a BAdI

BAdIs are based on object-oriented programming (OOP) concepts. It isn't necessary to understand OOP to make use of a BAdI, however. For simplicity, think of a method as a function module with import and export parameters that is executed at a specific time.

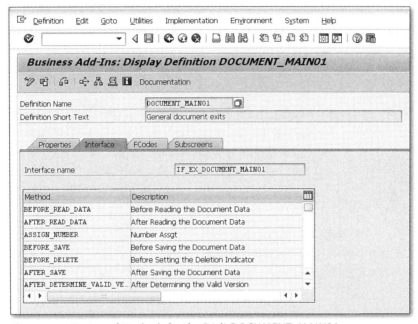

Figure 11.1 Review of Methods for the BAdI DOCUMENT_MAIN01

User exit functionality

To review the functionality of a user exit, as shown in Figure 11.2, use Transaction SMOD (SAP Enhancements). You should pay special attention to the available components. They will guide you to the function modules where you can quickly identify where custom code can be placed. For example, the user exit CV000001 (check-in enhancement for document management) has two components. The first function module, EXIT_SAPLCV00_001, allows you to make adjustments during check-in of files before the file is transported to the SAP system. The second function module, EXIT_SAPLCV00_002, allows you to make adjustments after the file has been transported to the SAP system. Each function module will have a Z* include where custom code can be included.

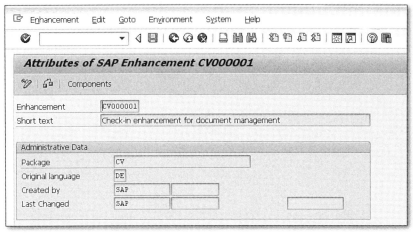

Figure 11.2 Review of User Exit CV000001 in Transaction SMOD

11.2 BAdIs Relevant to SAP DMS

SAP provides a number of BAdIs for your use. Listed in Table 11.1 are some BAdIs delivered by SAP that you'll commonly use during a project. Familiarizing yourself with these BAdIs will allow you to extend SAP DMS capabilities to meet your business requirements.

> **Tip**
>
> Most BAdIs related to SAP DMS, SAP Easy DMS, and the CAD Desktop can be found via Transaction SE18 by searching with the following patterns in the BAdI name:
> - *DOCUMENT*
> - *EASYDMS*
> - *CDESK*

BAdI	Description
DOCUMENT_AUTH01	Adds additional customer authorization checks.
DOCUMENT_BROWSER	Connects the SAP_APPL UI to the SAP Easy Document Management browser.

Table 11.1 Commonly Used BAdIs and Their Descriptions

BAdI	Description
DOCUMENT_ECL01	In connection with using the SAP ECL viewer and the viewer's stamping functionality, adds additional information from the document information record to the stamp. As part of the ECL viewer, there is a comparison function with which you can restrict or preselect which files should be available for comparison.
DOCUMENT_FILES01	Carries out additional customer checks so you can process original files associated to the document information record.
DOCUMENT_MAIN01	Includes various general methods to support additional processing of documents, including before save and after save methods.
DOCUMENT_MAIN02	Includes document exits for process after input (PAI)/ process before input (PBO) in Transactions CV01N/CV02N/CV03N.
DOCUMENT_NUMBER01	Provides additional checks when assigning document number, part, and version.
DOCUMENT_OBJ	Supports enhancement of object link function/page on the document information record. Executed for a variety of functions, including getting and setting data on screen, when jumping to other transactions, and before call of the function.
DOCUMENT_OBJ1	Supports enhancement of the object link function/page on the document information record. Executed before call of functions in PAI, before inserting new document, and setting cursor.
DOCUMENT_OBJ2	Supports enhancement of the object link function/page on the document information record. Executed when updating the object links on the document information record.
DOCUMENT_OFFINTEGR01	Controls or enhances the Microsoft Office integration that is used to display or change original files.

Table 11.1 Commonly Used BAdIs and Their Descriptions (Cont.)

BAdI	Description
DOCUMENT_PROC01	Limits what processes are listed when the PROCESSES button is used in Transaction CV04N (Find Document).
DOCUMENT_SEARCH01	Supports influencing search results before they are displayed in Transaction (Find Document).
DOCUMENT_STATUS01	Triggers additional actions or performs specific system checks before or after the status of the document information record is set.
DOCUMENT_STORAGE01	Performs additional checks or actions before or after check-in/check-out of original application files that are associated to the document information record.
DOCUMENT_SYSTEM01	Supports enhancement of general SAP DMS functions, including defining the frontend type.
DOCUMENT_THUMBNAIL	Includes enhancements for thumbnail display.
DOCUMENT_WEB01 DMS	Filters original files to retrieve the URL for check-out of an original file.
CDESK_BADI_MAIN	Changes data from CAD Desktop functions.
CDESK_ADD_FUNCTION	Adds additional functions to the CDESK interface.
CONVERTER_MAIN01	After a conversion process, updates or applies additional actions such as changing data before the results of the conversion process are stored.
EASYDMS	Enhances SAP Easy DMS capabilities.
EASYDMS_MAIN01	Enhances SAP Easy DMS, including but not limited to the following capabilities: ▸ Display or hide root folders for individual users. ▸ Create folders in SAP Easy DMS with predefined parameters. ▸ Generate URLs for document information records. ▸ Copy folder structure. ▸ Export folder structure. ▸ Get active object link tabs.

Table 11.1 Commonly Used BAdIs and Their Descriptions (Cont.)

11 | SAP DMS BAdIs and User Exits

PLM 7.01 and available BAdIs

> **Tip**
>
> Some of the BAdIs mentioned in the preceding table aren't executed when working with SAP PLM 7.01 and later releases. The best way to find out if the BAdIs are executed is to test via a breakpoint in the BAdI implementation/method you would like to use. You need to use an external breakpoint to do this. After the breakpoint is set, run the function in SAP PLM 7.0X DMS. If your breakpoint is activated, you'll know that SAP PLM 7.0X DMS is calling the BAdI as part of overall processing. If not, you need to look to see where you might include additionally capabilities as part of the SAP PLM 7.01 DMS Web Dynpro framework.

We'll review key BAdIs in detail in the upcoming sections. The BAdIs being reviewed are the ones that have been most commonly used during projects. For those being reviewed, we'll cover available methods, time of execution, and example usage. For BAdIs not being reviewed, the best place to learn more is in the BAdI definition itself. Additionally, you may also search SAP Help for further details.

11.2.1 BAdI DOCUMENT_MAIN01: General Document Processing

Using BAdI DOCUMENT_MAIN01, you can carry out customer-specific checks or actions during the process of reading or saving a document information record. This is a key BAdI that you'll use often because it allows you to check or manipulate document information data during these processes.

In Table 11.2, you'll find the available methods, time of execution, and example usages for BAdI DOCUEMENT_MAIN01.

Method	Time of Execution	Example Usage
Before_Read_Data	Before reading a document information record	Complete an additional authorization check to make sure that the user has access to display, change, or create.
After_Read_Data	After reading a document information record	Set lab/office or other default values in the document information record based on the location stored in the user's master record.

Table 11.2 Available Methods, Time of Execution, and Example Usage for BAdI DOCUMENT_MAIN01

Method	Time of Execution	Example Usage
Assign_Number	When saving a document information record	Determine the number to be assigned to the document information record. This replaces GET_NUMBER in Program MCDOKZNR.
Before_Save	Before saving a document information record	Perform a custom check to ensure that the document information record is linked to a material master before allowing the status to move to Released.
Before_Delete	Before deleting a document information record	Check additional rules contained in a Z-table before allowing the document to be deleted.
After_Save	After saving a document information record	Create a companion material master with the document number as the material number, and link it to the document information record.
After_Determine_Valid_Version	After a valid version has been determined	Perform a customer-specific check to determine the valid version of the document information record.

Table 11.2 Available Methods, Time of Execution, and Example Usage for BAdI DOCUMENT_MAIN01 (Cont.)

11.2.2 BAdI DOCUMENT_THUMBNAIL: Enhancement for Thumbnails

Using BAdI DOCUMENT_THUMBNAIL, you can adjust the display of the thumbnail image associated with the document information record. This includes adding additional text or changing the URL for displaying the thumbnail. Available methods, time of execution, and example usage for BAdI DOCUMENT_THUMBNAIL are outlined in Table 11.3.

Method	Time of Execution	Example Usage
Text displayed with thumbnail (overview)	Before display of thumbnail image	Create the text that is displayed for a thumbnail.
Change URL for displaying thumbnail	Before display of thumbnail image	Override the display of thumbnails that is defined in Customizing for a document.

Table 11.3 Available Methods, Time of Execution, and Example Usage for BAdI DOCUMENT_THUMBNAIL

11.2.3 BAdI DOCUMENT_AUTH01: Checking Authorization from the DMS

Using BAdI `DOCUMENT_AUTH01`, you can add customer authorization checks beyond the standard SAP authorization objects. This BAdI allows you to perform multiple additional custom checks to ensure that only an authorized individual gains access to documents. Going beyond standard authorization checks is often required due to business requirements. For example, you may not want to use authorization groups because of the requirements associated with maintaining roles and assigning these roles to users. Instead, you can develop a custom authorization check that will check a customer table for certain values to confirm that a user can open a document information record.

Available method, time of execution, and example usage for BAdI `DOCUMENT_AUTH01` are outlined in Table 11.4.

Method	Time of Execution	Example Usage
Check_Authority	After the following authorizations have been checked: C_DRAW_TCD C_DRAW_TCS C_DRAW_DOK	Customer-specific authorization check that goes beyond the checks performed by the standard authorization objects provided by SAP

Table 11.4 Available Method, Time of Execution, and Example Usage for BAdI DOCUMENT_AUTH01

11.2.4 BAdI DOCUMENT_FILES01: Processing of Original Application Files

BAdI `DOCUMENT_FILES01` allows you to carry out additional customer checks so you can process original files associated to the document information record. This is useful if you require special handling of original files during processing of a document information record. Additional checks can be made during or after assignment, before or after start of the application, and when creating a new version. This gives you an idea of when you can institute special processing instructions.

Available methods, time of execution, and example usage for BAdI `DOCUMENT_FILES01` are outlined in Table 11.5.

Method	Time of Execution	Example Usage
`Before_Assign_File`	Before assignment of an original application file	Restrict the type of application file that can be associated to a document information record.
`After_Assign_File`	After assignment of an original application file	Configure additional settings in the document information record after successful assignment of an original file.
`Before_Start_Appl`	Before starting the application that presents the original file	Uncompress a compressed file before starting the application.
`After_Start_Appl`	After the presenting application has started	Delete any temporary files stored on the frontend computer.
`Before_Copy_File_Dialog`	When creating a new version and the original application files aren't checked in before the dialog box for entering a copy path is displayed	Determine the file name for the new version.

Table 11.5 Available Methods, Time of Execution, and Example Usage for BAdI DOCUMENT_FILES01

Method	Time of Execution	Example Usage
After_Copy_File_Dialog	When creating a new version, and the original application files aren't checked in after the original application files were copied	Confirm that an original application file exists.
Generate_Copy_File_Name	When creating a new version, and the original application files aren't checked in and before the standard process for generating file names is run	Generate or change the name of the original file when creating a new version of the document information record.

Table 11.5 Available Methods, Time of Execution, and Example Usage for BAdI DOCUMENT_FILES01 (Cont.)

11.2.5 BAdI DOCUMENT_STORAGE01: Transport of Original Application Files

BAdI DOCUMENT_STORAGE01 lets you perform additional checks or actions before or after check-in/check-out of original application files that are associated to the document information record.

Available methods, time of execution, and example usage for this BAdI are outlined in Table 11.6.

Method	Time of Execution	Example Usage
Before_Checkin	Before physical check-in of an original application file	Compress the original file being checked in.
After_Checkin	After physical check-in of an original application file	Automatically set the status of the document information record to a review state, such as Pending Review. Setting this status may trigger a review workflow.

Table 11.6 Available Methods, Time of Execution, and Example Usage for BAdI DOCUMENT_STORAGE01

Method	Time of Execution	Example Usage
Before_Checkout	Before physical check-out of an original application file when displaying, changing, or copying the file; also executed for original files that are not checked in	Adjust the file name before it reaches the frontend computer.
Before_List_Storagecat	Before the display of the possible storage categories when checking in an original file	Filter the list of possible storage categories based on the user's location.

Table 11.6 Available Methods, Time of Execution, and Example Usage for BAdI DOCUMENT_STORAGE01 (Cont.)

11.2.6 BAdI DOCUMENT_STATUS01: Status Checks

Using BAdI DOCUMENT_STATUS01, you can trigger additional actions or perform specifics system checks before or after the status of the document information record is set.

Available methods, time of execution, and example usage for this BAdI are outlined in Table 11.7.

Method	Time of Execution	Example Usage
After_Change_Status	After every status change	Execute a custom report when a document information record reaches a status of Released. The report output is then linked to the document information record.
Before_List_Status	Before the list of possible statuses is displayed	Complete additional checks beyond standard configuration for which statuses are possible and selectable by users.

Table 11.7 Available Methods, Time of Execution, and Example Usage for BAdI DOCUMENT_STATUS01

11.2.7 BAdI DOCUMENT_MAIN02: Document Exits and Menu Enhancements

BAdI DOCUMENT_MAIN02 lets you check menu enhancements at the point in time of PAI.

Checks are executed with the following transactions:

- Create Document (Transaction CV01N)
- Change Document (Transaction CV02N)
- Display Document (Transaction CV03N)

Available interfaces, time of execution, and example usage for this BAdI are outlined in Table 11.8.

Interface	Time of Execution	Example Usage
D100_Before_PAI	Before the actual PAI of screen 100	Additional checks when selecting a function in DMS
D101_Before_PAI	Before the actual PAI of screen 101	Additional checks when selecting a function in DMS
D100_PAI_CU1	PAI for menu enhancement 1 (+D100_CU1) screen 100	Processing of menu enhancements
D100_PAI_CU2	PAI for menu enhancement 1 (+D100_CU2) screen 100	Processing of menu enhancements
D100_PAI_CU3	PAI for menu enhancement 1 (+D100_CU3) screen 100	Processing of menu enhancements
D100_PAI_CU1	PAI for menu enhancement 1 (+D100_CU1) screen 101	Processing of menu enhancements
D101_PAI_CU2	PAI for menu enhancement 1 (+D100_CU2) screen 101	Processing of menu enhancements
D101_PAI_CU3	PAI for menu enhancement 1 (+D100_CU3) screen 101	Processing of menu enhancements

Table 11.8 Available Interfaces, Time of Execution, and Example Usage for BAdI DOCUMENT_MAN02

11.2.8 BAdI DOCUMENT_NUMBER01: Checking the Attributes of the Document Key

Using BAdI `DOCUMENT_NUMBER01`, you can perform additional checks on key attributes associated with the document information record. This includes checks for the document number, document version, document part, and getting the next and last version.

Available interfaces, time of execution, and example usage for this BAdI are outlined in Table 11.9.

Interface	Time of Execution	Example Usage
DOCNUMBER_Check	Before standard checks are carried out by SAP DMS	Carry out an additional check for the assignment of a document number.
DOCVERSION_Check	Before standard checks are carried out by SAP DMS	Carry out an additional check for the assignment of a document version.
DOCPART_Check	Before standard checks are carried out by SAP DMS	Carry out an additional check for the assignment of a document part.
DOCVERSION_Get_Next	When creating a new version of a document	Get the next version of a document information record. Beyond basic determination, this may include additional rules for determination.
DOCVERSION_Get_Last	When creating a new version of a document	Determine the last version of a document information record.

Table 11.9 Available Methods, Time of Execution, and Example Usage for BAdI DOCUMENT_NUMBER01

11.2.9 BAdI: DOCUMENT_PROC01: Filter for SAP DMS Processes

BAdI `DOCUMENT_PROC01` lets you limit what processes are listed when the PROCESSES button is used in Transaction CV04N (Find Document). A *process* is defined as an action that you can take on a selected set of document information records returned by executing the Find Document transaction.

For example, you might set the deletion indicator on execution of the process for the selected document information records.

Available interfaces, time of execution, and example usage for BAdI `DOCUMENT_PROC01` are outlined in Table 11.10.

Interface	Time of Execution	Example Usage
Before_List_Process	Before displaying a list of processes	Based on the user's location, only list certain processes that can be executed.
Before_List_Status	Not implemented in current releases	N/A

Table 11.10 Available Interfaces, Time of Execution, and Example Usage for BAdI DOCUMENT_PROC01

11.2.10 BAdI DOCUMENT_WEB01: Enhancements for the DMS@Web Scenarios

You can use BAdI `DOCUMENT_WEB01` to filter original files and to retrieve the URL for check-out of an original file.

Available interfaces, time of execution, and example usage for this BAdI are outlined in Table 11.11.

Interface	Time of Execution	Example Usage
Filter_Files	Before transferring document data to the Internet Transaction Server (ITS)	Check original application files in the web scenario.
Get_URL	N/A	Determine URL for check-out in the web.

Table 11.11 Available Interfaces, Time of Execution, and Example Usage for BAdI DOCUMENT_WEB01

11.2.11 BAdI DOCUMENT_OFFINTEGR01: Enhancements for Microsoft Office Integration

Using BAdI `DOCUMENT_OFFINTEGR01`, you can control or enhance the Microsoft Office integration that is used to display or change original files.

Available interfaces, time of execution, and example usage of this BAdI are outlined in Table 11.12.

Interface	Time of Execution	Example Usage
`Edit_Link_Items`	Before data is transferred from SAP to the Office application. (Word, Excel, etc.)	Transfer additional data from the SAP system to the Office application.
`After_Open`	After opening an original application file in an Office application	When viewing, set an additional attribute in the document information record that lists information such as the date and time the file was opened.
`Read_Class`	When reading the classification of the Office integration	N/A
`Edit_Form_Items`	After opening the Office application, to transfer data from the SAP system to the Office application	Transfer additional data from a material master or other object that is related to the document information record.

Table 11.12 Available Interfaces, Time of Execution, and Example Usage for BAdI DOCUMENT_OFFINTEGR01

11.2.12 BAdI DOCUMENT_ECL01: Displaying Original Application Files with the Viewer

With BAdI `DOCUMENT_ECL01`, in connection with using the SAP ECL viewer and the viewer's stamping functionality, you can add additional information from the document information record to the stamp. Also, in the viewer's comparison tool, you can restrict or preselect which files should be available for comparison.

Available interfaces, time of execution, and example usage for this BAdI are outlined in Table 11.13.

Interface	Time of Execution	Example Usage
Show_Doc_Meta_Data	Before stamping of viewable file	Transfer additional information from the document information record to be included in the stamping of a viewable file.
Before_List_Docs_To_Add	Before generating the selection list in the SELECT ORIGINAL dialog box	Based on business rules, preselect or restrict which documents are added to the SELECT ORIGINAL dialog box.

Table 11.13 Available Interfaces, Time of Execution, and Example Usage for BAdI DOCUMENT_ECL01

11.2.13 BAdI CONVERTER_MAIN01: Exits during Conversion

Using BAdI CONVERTER_MAIN01, after a conversion process, you can update or apply additional actions such as changing data before the results of the conversion process are stored.

Available interfaces, time of execution, and example usage for this BAdI are outlined in Table 11.14.

Interface	Time of Execution	Example Usage
Checkin_Change_WS_Application	After the conversion process has run	Change the workstation application associated to the original file before check-in.
Checkin_Before_Checkin	After the conversion process has run	Change the description, storage category, or other data element before check-in of file.
Checkin_After_Checkin	After the conversion process has run	Delete files after check-in.

Table 11.14 Available Interfaces, Time of Execution, and Example Usage for BAdI CONVERTER_MAIN01

11.3 User Exits Available in SAP DMS

In this chapter, greater emphasis is placed on BAdIs than user exits because most SAP DMS enhancements can be carried out using one of the BAdIs. However, there are a number of useful user exits, specifically in the area of document distribution. As you can see in Table 11.15, user exits CVDI0001 through CVDI0020 are all related to document distribution. Therefore, these can be used when enhancing this functionality. As an example, you can use user exit CVDI0003 to determine which original files should be sent with a distribution order.

Exit	Description
CV000001	Check-in enhancement for document management
CV110001	DMS: Enhancements for DMS dialog
CVDI0001	User exit: Document Distribution (DDS) – Save recipient list
CVDI0002	User exit: DDS – Modify initial values for screen 100
CVDI0003	User exit: DDS – Determine original
CVDI0004	User exit: DDS – Determine document part and version
CVDI0005	User exit: DDS – Create distribution order
CVDI0006	User exit: DDS – Check part order
CVDI0007	User exit: DDS – Create initial order
CVDI0008	User exit: DDS – Determine context
CVDI0009	User exit: DDS – Access to ITS
CVDI0010	User exit: DDS – Determine workstation application
CVDI0011	User exit: DDS – ITS access to all distribution packages
CVDI0020	User exit: For distributing originals
CVDS0001	User exit: For ALE DMS (DOCMAS)

Table 11.15 Available SAP DMS User Exits

11.4 Enhancement of SAP DMS in PLM 7.01

With the release of SAP PLM 7.01, a new web-based framework for SAP DMS has been created. The web framework has its own set of BAdIs to support enhancements. As mentioned earlier, the web framework doesn't always respect the classic BAdIs that work within the SAP GUI. Testing needs to be done to ensure which ones are respected. You can carry out a test by creating a simple implementation of the BAdI and adding an external breakpoint to the method you want to use. If the breakpoint is triggered, you'll know you can use this BAdI. Listed in Table 11.16 are a few of the BAdIs available to support enhancement of the SAP PLM 7.01 version of SAP DMS.

BAdI	Description
/PLMI/CL_EX_DIR_LINK	Implement customer-specific object types linked to a document information record. This BAdI is called when handling object links.
/PLMI/IF_EX_DIR_THMB	Implement a customer-specific search for a thumbnail.
/PLMI/CL_DIR_BRW_EXPL_SETNGS	Define a specific explosion setting for the document browser.

Table 11.16 Additional BAdIs Available with SAP PLM 7.01.

11.5 Summary

In this chapter, we reviewed the use of SAP BAdIs and user exits. We defined the methods/interfaces, time of execution, and example usage for each BAdI and looked at the available and related user exists. By utilizing BAdIs or user exits, you can enhance the system to include functionality that isn't delivered through standard IMG configuration. It's often the case during projects that a business requirement will go beyond the standard configuration. When this occurs, you can use the information in this chapter to develop a solution.

In the next chapter, we'll briefly review what we've covered in this book and address the future of SAP DMS.

This chapter reviews what you've learned throughout this book and discusses the future of SAP DMS.

12 Conclusion

Congratulations on arriving at the conclusion of this book. At this point, you've spent a good deal of time studying and learning about SAP DMS. In this chapter, we'll provide you with a chapter-by-chapter review of what you've learned by reading this book, with brief highlights and key points for each chapter. At the end of the chapter, we'll give you an idea of what SAP DMS might look like in the future.

12.1 SAP DMS: Now You Know It

In this section, we'll briefly recap what you've learned in each chapter of this book.

12.1.1 Introduction

After reading through Chapter 1, you developed the skills to evaluate whether SAP DMS is right for you and what SAP DMS can offer your business. From this introduction, you should understand that SAP DMS is an enterprise document management system available in your base SAP system. We took a look at some of the benefits of implementing SAP DMS, including secure storage for documents, full-text search across documents, and the ability to classify documents for searching. After learning about SAP DMS benefits, you learned how to judge the complexity of your project by looking at the volume of different types of documents you plan to manage with SAP DMS, making sure to take the types of resources required for a project into consideration. Finally, you learned about the availability of SAP DMS across different releases.

Chapter 1

12.1.2 Questions to Answer before Starting Your SAP DMS Project

Chapter 2 In Chapter 2, you learned that document management is not simply about storing files, but that instead it's important to answer key questions about your SAP DMS project before moving on to actual system activities. This way you have a firm idea of the goals you want to achieve with SAP DMS. In this chapter, you reviewed which documents should be defined and managed in SAP DMS. You also considered how you want to search for documents and what attributes are necessary to meet these requirements. You learned that structure and attributes must exist on which you can search to find documents. Reading this chapter, you obtained the skills and insight to start defining your requirements so that when you learned the basic functions and configuration activities, you were able to tailor the system to your requirements.

12.1.3 SAP DMS Step-by-Step Instructions

Chapter 3 In Chapter 3, you learned how to execute the basic SAP DMS transactions. This includes the transactions to create, change, and display document information records. You also learned about additional transactions to execute document searches and classification searches, and you reviewed the product structure browser. Knowledge of these items is helpful before moving on to the configuration activities. By learning how to create a document information record, you also learned about document types, additional attributes, and statuses. Knowing how these items relate to other items in the system makes the configuration activity much clearer.

12.1.4 Configuring SAP DMS

Chapter 4 Beyond learning how to operate the basic transactions of SAP DMS, Chapter 4 covered the next most important topic, configuration. Configuration lets you set up SAP DMS to meet your business requirements. With the configuration items complete, you were able to use SAP DMS and move on to additional topics such as defining your security requirements and enhancing the system through the use of SAP-provide BAdIs.

12.1.5 Infrastructure Requirements

In Chapter 5, you learned about the different infrastructure pieces available to support your SAP DMS projects. The infrastructure pieces are underlying system elements that make SAP DMS possible but are invisible to the user. They include the content, cache, TREX, and conversion servers. Each infrastructure piece fulfills a unique requirement important for SAP DMS. You also learned about different architecture options. A simple architecture involves a single content server that covers all of your requirements. If you have a more complex environment with people at multiple locations accessing and creating data, you can install multiple content and cache servers, creating a more complex environment. What a complex environment ultimately looks like depends on the number of users, locations being served, and how your WAN is structured.

Chapter 5

12.1.6 SAP DMS Security

At the beginning of Chapter 6, you learned about questions to consider when defining your SAP DMS security scheme. These helped you understand and define your security requirements. You also learned about the different authorization objects that SAP provides for creating a security scheme. Finally, there was a discussion of how to use a specific BAdI to create a customer-specific authorization check using ABAP.

Chapter 6

12.1.7 Frontends to SAP DMS

In Chapter 7, you learned about three different frontends: WebDocuments, SAP Easy DMS, and the SAP DMS Portal iView. Frontends are important because they offer a different user experience—possibly simpler—for accessing and executing SAP DMS functionalities than using the SAP GUI. Users of these frontends might include persons that are classified as consumers of information. They are individuals who are looking for easy ways to get at the information in SAP DMS, rather than creating and changing information in the system. The frontend interfaces work using the same configuration as SAP DMS; therefore, when you have your base SAP DMS configuration working in the SAP GUI, you can start working with the different frontends to see if the user experience is appropriate for you and your users.

Chapter 7

12.1.8 SAP PLM 7.02 DMS WebUI

Chapter 8 — In Chapter 8, you learned about the capabilities of the SAP PLM WebUI in relation to DMS. You now have a good understanding of the capabilities, including the difference between the SAP GUI and WebUI. You also are now familiar with working within the SAP PLM 7.02 environment, including using the personal object work list, process routes, and access control management for securing documents. In addition, you learned the configuration options in the SAP PLM 7.02 environment related to SAP DMS.

12.1.9 Integrating a CAD System to SAP DMS

Chapter 9 — In Chapter 9, you learned that it's possible to integrate your CAD system to SAP DMS. CAD systems you can integrate include AutoCAD, CATIA, UG NX, and Pro/Engineer. You also saw some of the benefits of integrating a CAD system to SAP, including secure data storage, the ability to execute SAP DMS transactions directly from a CAD system, and the ability to use SAP Engineering Change Management tools to control updates to CAD data. You also learned about the CAD Desktop, which is the tool provided by SAP for management of CAD data within the SAP GUI. Finally, you walked through a sample scenario to learn about the steps involved in working with a CAD integration.

12.1.10 Simple Document Approval Process using SAP Workflow

Chapter 10 — In Chapter 10, you learned how to create a basic document approval workflow so that you can build on this example to create more complex workflows. The concepts covered included how to build a workflow definition, what triggering events and container elements are, and how to activate and test your workflow after it has been built. The combination of SAP DMS and SAP Workflow can be powerful in that it lets you automate approval/review processes and an unlimited number of additional business processes.

12.1.11 SAP DMS BAdIs and User Exits

Chapter 11 taught you about going beyond basic SAP DMS configuration by using BAdIs and user exits provided by SAP to enhance SAP DMS. You learned a number of different BAdIs, and how and why they are superior to user exits. For each BAdI, you learned about the different methods and time of execution, and saw an example of usage. Although BAdIs typically address most requirements, a number of helpful user exits also exist for document distribution and ALE.

Chapter 11

12.2 The Future of SAP DMS

Looking into the SAP crystal ball can be difficult. However, with SAP DMS, there are some clues as to where it will head in the future. One thing you can look for are additional frontends to SAP DMS to further enhance the user experience, including the development of mobile applications for viewing and creating documents and additional enhancements in the capabilities of SAP PLM 7.02 DMS functions. Users are always looking for easier ways to get documents and data stored into the SAP system and likely, SAP DMS will become more integrated into applications, such as the Microsoft Office suite. This gives users the ability to interact with SAP DMS directly from the applications they use to create data, lowering the number of clicks needed to store data, and moving further away from a traditional GUI interface. Fewer clicks make users feel less like they are working with an SAP system, and as a result, the acceptance level goes up.

12.3 Summary

In this chapter, we provided you with a look back on what you've learned by reading this book and how it fits into the big picture of your projects. We've covered a lot of material on different subjects and topics; if you've judiciously studied the content of this book, you now have all of the tools you need to use and configure SAP DMS.

We hope that you've enjoyed reading and have gained useful insight into SAP DMS. SAP DMS is an important tool for you and your organization, and now you know how to put this tool to use.

Appendices

A Glossary 261
B Review of Menu Items 265
C The Author 271

A   Glossary

Knowing the terminology used in SAP DMS will be helpful as you work through your SAP DMS project. The following terms and their definitions are used most frequently in SAP DMS.

authorization group   An authorization group is used, among other options, to control access to documents. It consists of a four-character alphanumeric identifier. If an authorization group is assigned to a document information record, the user must have this authorization group in his security profile.

access control list (ACL)   Set on the AUTHORIZATIONS tab of the document information record, this indicates security or access rules for the document.

access control management (ACM)   As part of SAP PLM 7.0 and later releases, you can use ACM to control access to documents and other objects.

cache server   The cache server is a designated server that keeps a cached copy of original files as they are pulled for viewing or change. It's usually located at a remote location that doesn't have a content server. Requests from the remote location to view documents will go first to the cache server and then to the content server where the original file is located. The goal is to help reduce network usage.

CAD indicator   The CAD indicator is located on a document information record to show whether a document information record has been created or changed through a CAD interface to SAP DMS.

CAD interface   A CAD interface allows you to interface a CAD system directly to SAP DMS. For example, SAP offers CAD interfaces to interface AutoCAD, UG, CATIA, and Pro/E directly to SAP DMS. Using these interfaces, certain SAP DMS functions can be carried out directly in the CAD system.

change number   A change number is an engineering change master or engineering change request/order used to control the creation and change of document information records.

content server   A content server stores original files that are checked into SAP DMS. This server is separate from the main SAP DMS. There can be one or many content servers associated with an instance of SAP DMS.

content version   If configured, SAP DMS will store a copy of the original file each time it's stored back in the system after being checked out. This copy of the original file is referred to as a content version.

conversion server   The conversion server is a dedicated server that converts original files stored with a document information record into a neutral format such as TIF or PDF. A conversion can be triggered based on a status change. The conversion processes are controlled through IMG configuration.

Created in CAD indicator   This indicates that the document information record was created from one of the CAD integrations.

deletion indicator   The deletion indicator on a document information record indicates whether the document information record should be deleted from the system. Deletion is carried out through Program MCDOKDEL.

document browser   In this browser, you can select your documents via a folder structure. The folder structure is created directly in the document browser or via SAP Easy DMS.

document description   A document description describes the document that is being stored. It consists of 40 characters.

document distribution   A document distribution is a system used to distribute documents from the DMS. Documents are distributed according to different criteria (e.g., communication type and context).

document information record   The document information record in SAP DMS contains attributes that describe the original file being stored. Attributes include owner, status, short description, authorization group, and attributes that are defined through configuration.

document key   The document key consists of four elements:

- Document number
- Document type
- Document part
- Document version

These four elements together make up the document key. For example: 1000000/DRW/000/00.

document number   The document number is a unique ID for each document information record. It can be internally or externally generated, and it can consist of numbers or a combination of numbers and letters. The document number is an element of the document key. Some examples include the following:

- Numeric: 10000003236
- Alphanumeric: Spec10001
- Alpha: SpecF150

document owner   The document owner is the person who is responsible for the document information record. At initial creation, the name of the creator is placed into the USER field on the document information record. When a document is updated, the name in the USER field is updated with the name of the individual making the change.

document part   The document part is a section of a document that is maintained as an independent document. Design departments, for example, can use document parts to divide large documents, such as design drawings, into pages. The document part is an element of the document key.

document retention Document retention is a part of the overall records management policy and relates to the time a document should be kept or retained.

document status The document status identifies where a document information record is at in its lifecycle. Example statuses include In Work and Released. The document status controls items such as security, and it triggers processes such as automated document conversions.

Document Structure indicator The DOCUMENT STRUCTURE indicator specifies whether the document information record has an associated document structure. A document structure is similar to a BOM. Functions to process the document structure can be accessed under the ENVIRONMENT menu item in the document information record.

document type The document type is a high-level categorization of a group of documents. It consists of a three-character alphanumeric identifier and is an element of the document key. An example of a document type is DRW.

document version The document version is a number or letter that identifies a document's version. It is an element of the document key.

ECL viewer The ECL viewer is provided by SAP for viewing a variety of 2D and 3D formats. Using the viewer for a specific file format is controlled through IMG configuration.

frontend type Frontend types, also called data carriers, are defined through IMG configuration. The data carrier controls how original files will be processed on a local machine. This concept is important when you go through the IMG activity DEFINE WORKSTATION APPLICATION. When defining how an application should start for an original file, this definition is associated to a data carrier.

index server The index server is a dedicated server that indexes documents stored in a content server for the full-text search functionality to work. The index server is implemented via the SAP TREX technology.

lab office The lab office is the design office, laboratory, or location that is responsible for the document being stored. Values for lab office are controlled through material master configuration.

neutral file A neutral file is generated out of an automated conversion process. Conversion takes place on a conversion server. This is usually a TIF or PDF file.

object links Through the OBJECT LINKS tab in the document information record, you can link a document information record to many other objects in the SAP system. This is important because it provides a way to link supporting documentation to these other objects. For example, let's say that a company stored specifications using SAP DMS. Through object linking, it's possible to link the specifications to related material masters.

original file   An original file is an application file that is associated to a document information record. One or many original files can be attached to a document information record.

process route   This tool in SAP PLM 7.01 allows you to send out ad hoc workflow tasks for a specific document information record.

redline and markup   Redline and markup is the process of using the redlining and markup tools in the ECL Viewer to make annotations to a file that is stored using SAP DMS. Redline and markup can occur on file formats such as TIF and PDF.

revision   A revision is a single-character field that identifies the revision of a document. The REVISION field is available only when using a change number associated to the document information record.

right hemisphere (RH) file   This is a lightweight 3D file generated from the SAP Visual Enterprise Generator from CAD data stored within SAP. RH files can be viewed with the SAP Visual Enterprise Viewer.

SAP Easy DMS   This is a tool that integrates the SAP DMS functions directly into Microsoft Windows Explorer, including the use of folders, drag and drop, and a variety of other functions that are familiar to users of Windows.

SAP Visual Enterprise Viewer   The SAP Visual Enterprise viewer is provided by SAP for viewing a variety of 2D and 3D formats. It is used with SAP PLM 7.0 and later releases.

status network   The status network is the lifecycle of the document information record. An example status network is as follows: A document information record starts in the status of In Work. It then can be set to a status of Being Checked. From the Being Checked status, it can be set to Released, or it can go back to In Work. Through IMG configuration, you can build a status network for each document type.

status log   The status log is a record of when a status was set on a document information record. It also includes a short comment from the user setting the status. This comment can be configured to be mandatory, optional, or bypassed, based on IMG configuration.

superior document   On the GENERAL DATA tab of the document information record, you can relate the document information record to another superior document information record.

valid from   This is the date from which the document is valid. The valid from date is controlled from the change master associated with the document information record.

workstation application   A workstation application is defined to start when viewing or changing an original file associated to a document information record.

B   Review of Menu Items

This appendix provides you with an overview of the menu options in SAP DMS transactions (as circled in Figure B.1), as well as descriptions for each of the menu items that appear below each option.

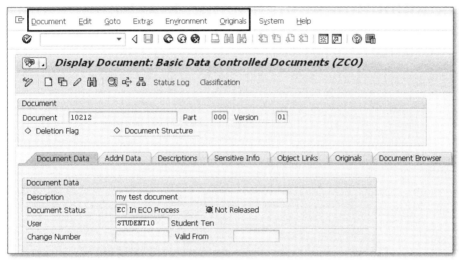

Figure B.1 Menu Options in SAP DMS Transactions

B.1   Menu Option Document

Menu Item	Description
OTHER DOCUMENT	Open another document information record.
CREATE	Create a new document information record.
CHANGE	If in display mode, switch to change mode.
DISPLAY	If in change mode, switch to display mode.

Menu Item	Description
FIND	Open the Find Document transaction (Transaction CV04N).
NEW VERSION	Create a new version of the current document information record.
SAVE	Save the document information record.
CHANGE DELETION IND.	Set the deletion indicator on the document information record. The actual deletion of a document information record is carried out through Program MCDOKDEL.
EXIT	Exit the current transaction.

B.2 Menu Option Edit

Menu Item	Description
CANCEL	Cancel the transaction.

B.3 Menu Option Goto

Menu Item	Description
MESSAGES	Display messages.
BACK	Back out of the transaction.

B.4 Menu Option Extras

Menu Item	Description
CLASSIFICATION	Display the classification information for the active document information record.

Menu Item	Description
VERSIONS	Display a list of versions for the active document information record.
DOCUMENT PARTS	Display a list of document parts for the active document information record.
SEQUENCE OF SOURCES	Show the sequence of sources, or from which document information record the active document information record was created.
HIERARCHY	If the document information record belongs to a hierarchy, display the report showing the document hierarchy.
STATUS NETWORK	Display the status network for the active document information record.
STATUS LOG	Display the status log for the active document information record.
SETTINGS	Set a working directory for an application.
CHANGE FRONT END TYPE	Change the frontend type. This is important when you're working on a client that is not Windows-based, such as a UNIX client. The frontend type controls how applications are launched when displaying or changing original files.

B.5   Menu Option Environment

Menu Item	Description
DISPLAY CHANGES	Display the change history report for the active document information record.

Menu Item	Description
REVISION LEVELS	Display the revision levels for the active document information record.
DOCUMENT WHERE USED	Execute a where-used report to check whether the document is used in a document structure.
PRODUCT STRUCTURE	Open the product structure browser with the context of the active document information record.
DOCUMENT STRUCTURE	Execute functions related to document structures.
DOCUMENT DISTRIBUTION	Execute functions related to document distribution.
DIGITAL SIGNATURES	Display digital signatures associated with the active document information record.
CHECK IN ARCHIVE	Store and associate an original file using the archive link functionality.
DISPLAY FROM ARCHIVE	Display an original file that was associated to the active document information record through an archive link.
COPY FROM ARCHIVE	Copy a document associated to the active document information record from an archive link.

B.6 Menu Option Originals

Menu Item	Description
CHECK IN ORIGINAL	Check in an original file.
CHECK IN AS	Check in an original file to a specific storage category.
CHECK IN AS NEW VERSION	Check in an original file as a new content version.

Menu Item	Description
PROCESS UNDER	Check out an original file to a location on a local machine.
COPY TO	Copy an original file to a location on a local machine. This is accomplished without checking out the file.
RESET CHECK-OUT	Cancel the checking out of a file. This is often helpful if a local file has been corrupted after check-out, and you want to return to the previously stored copy.

B.7 Additional Resources

For additional help on any of the menu items mentioned in this appendix, SAP Help provides a great deal of information. SAP Help can be accessed at *http://help.sap.com*.

You can find SAP DMS-specific help under the heading SAP ERP CENTRAL COMPONENT.

C   The Author

Eric Stajda is the Practice Lead at LeverX specializing in the area of SAP PLM. He has helped customers find and implement solutions in a variety of industries, including automotive, high-tech, pharmaceuticals, discrete manufacturing, and oil and gas. Most recently, he has been developing and deploying rapid prototyping techniques to help customers implement SAP PLM functionalities, including SAP DMS, in a faster, more cost-efficient manner. He is a regular speaker at SAP conferences, including ASUG, SAP Insider, and SAPPHIRE. He resides in the Detroit area, with his wife, Liz.

Please send email inquiries to: *eric.stajda@leverx.com*.

Linkedin Profile: *http://www.linkedin.com/in/estajda*.

Index

A

ABAP, 113
ABAP Objects, 235
Access control list, 136, 148, 185, 261
Access control management, 151, 180, 185, 261
ACO_SUPER, 151
Activities for documents, 137
Activities for recipient lists, 143
Additional attributes, 27, 44, 47, 86, 99
Additional Data tab, 65
Additional Files checkbox, 108
Addnl Data tab, 47
Adjusting the layout, 173
Advanced search, 191
Alternative Screen, 90
Application file, 31
Appl. Icon, 107
Archive identification field, 107
Archiving Authorization, 89
AScEx., 90
Attachments, 27
Authorization for class type, 145, 146
Authorization group, 136, 140, 261
Authorization objects, 136, 137
Authorizations tab, 185
AutoCAD, 79, 210, 214
AutoDesk Inventor, 210

B

Backup and restore, 121
BAdI, 235, 257
    CDESK_BADI_MAIN, 239
    CONVERTER_MAIN01, 239, 250
    DOCUMENT_AUTH01, 136, 237, 242
    DOCUMENT_BROWSER, 237
    DOCUMENT_ECL01, 238, 249
    DOCUMENT_FILES01, 238, 243
    Document_Main01, 235

BAdI (Cont.)
    DOCUMENT_MAIN01, 238, 240
    DOCUMENT_MAIN02, 238
    DOCUMENT_MAN02, 246
    DOCUMENT_NUMBER01, 238, 247
    DOCUMENT_OBJ, 238
    DOCUMENT_OBJ1, 238
    DOCUMENT_OBJ2, 238
    DOCUMENT_OFFINTEGR01, 238, 249
    DOCUMENT_PROC01, 239, 247
    DOCUMENT_SEARCH01, 239
    DOCUMENT_STATUS01, 239, 245
    DOCUMENT_STORAGE01, 239, 244
    DOCUMENT_SYSTEM01, 239
    DOCUMENT_THUMBNAIL, 239, 241
    DOCUMENT_WEB01, 248
    DOCUMENT_WEB01 DMS, 239
    EASYDMS, 239
    EASYDMS_MAIN01, 239
    /PLMI/CL_DIR_BRW_EXPL_SETNGS, 252
    /PLMI/CL_EX_DIR_LINK, 252
    /PLMI/IF_EX_DIR_THMB, 252
BCV, 192
Bill of material maintenance, 147
BMP, 79
BOM, 27
BOR Object Type category, 223
Business Context Viewer, 192
Business objects, 26
Business process, 26
Business role, 30
Business Server Page, 156
Business users, 22

C

Cache server, 35, 119, 122, 255, 261
    Customizing, 124
Cache size and deletion, 123

CAD, 209
 application, 27
 benefits, 210
 data, 35, 37
 data migration, 214
 Desktop, 209, 211
 drawings, 25, 27, 29, 31
 integration, 209
 integration scenario, 213
CAD indicator, 91, 261
CAD interface, 261
Calcomp, 79
CALS MIL-R
 Type I and Type II, 79
CATIA V4, 210
CATIA V5, 210, 214
CDESK_ADD_FUNCTION, 239
C_DRAD_OBJ, 141
C_DRAW_BGR, 137, 140
C_DRAW_DOK, 142
C_DRAW_STA, 139
C_DRAW_TCD, 137
C_DRAW_TCS, 137, 138
C_DRZA_TCD, 143
C_DRZI_TCD, 144
CGM, 79
Change control process, 29
Change Docs, 89
Change history, 32
Change number, 261
Characteristics, 100
Characteristic Values tab, 184
Check In, 93
C_KLAH_BKL, 146
Class, 75, 90
 Type, 75, 90, 100
Class characteristics, 76
Classes tab, 183
Classification Search, 43, 75
CM Relevance, 89
Comparison tool, 249
Condition builder, 224
Configuration in SAP IMG, 84
Configuration of WebDocuments, 157
Construction drawings, 36
Consumers, 36, 131
Container element, 220

Content server, 35, 119, 131, 255
 request, 120
 single, 132
Content version, 34, 93, 261
Content version checkbox, 108
Conversion, 37
Conversion process, 86, 239, 250
 Word to PDF, 127
Conversion scripts and tools, 128
Conversion server, 119, 127, 131, 255, 261
Created In Cad, 262
Create document, 179
Creating document types, 86
Creators, 131
CSProxyCache.INI, 123
C_STUE_BER, 147
C_TCLA_BKA, 145
Custom authorization check, 137
Customer authorization check, 153
CVAW_ENTIRE, 156

D

Data check off checkbox, 108
Data migration, 38
Default Appl., 90
Default class, 99, 102
Define
 laboratories/design offices, 103
 object links, 98
 profile, 115
 revision levels, 104
 workstation applications, 105
Define search sequence for viewable file, 199
Delete file after check-in, 108
Deletion Indicator, 69, 112
Description, 27
DGN, 79
Dialog when overwriting checkbox, 107
Digital signature, 29
Distribute originals, 76
Distribution order, 143
Distr. Lock, 93
Dis. WS applic., 90

Document access, 142
DOCUMENT_AUTH01, 153
Document Browser, 195, 262
Document Creators, 36
Document description, 262
Document distribution, 76, 262
Document hierarchy, 69
Document information record, 262
 copy, 69
 create, 44
 delete, 69
 search, 67
 searching for, 62
 versions, 62
Document key, 262
Document numbering, 32
Document owner, 262
Document part, 262
Document processing, 112
Document retention, 36, 263
Document status, 30, 136, 139, 263
Document structure, 71
 original file check, 71
Document Structure indicator, 263
Document type, 136, 218, 263
 configuration example, 88
 steps for configuration, 88
Document Type, 44, 89
 Description, 89
Document version, 263
Drag and drop, 164

E

ECL viewer, 238, 249, 263
Editing offline, 172
EDMICS C4, 79
Engineering change, 26
Engineering Change Management, 29, 91, 93
Enhancement package 5, 24
Enhancement package 6, 23
Event, 223
Example workstation application, 106
External Number Range, 90

F

File format field, 107
File Size, 90
File Suffix For Appl., 107
Fld. Sel., 94
Folder creation, 198
Folders in SAP Easy DMS, 170
Folder structure, 165
Formal approval process, 29
Form routine, 94
Frontend type, 263
 PC, 111
Full-text search, 34, 68, 126
 benefits, 125
Full-text search, 34

G

General task, 227
GIF, 79, 115

H

HPGL/HPGL-2, 79
HP ME 10/30 MI, 79
HTTP, 120

I

Icon for release status, 201
I-deas, 210
IGES, 79
Indexing process, 68
Index server, 263
Index server (TREX), 119, 125, 131
Infrastructure requirements, 119, 255
Initial status, 92
Initial version, 33
Integrated viewer, 109
Interface with external system, 37
Internal Number Range, 89
Internal viewer, 78

J

JPEG, 79
JPG, 115
JT
   Direct Model, 79

L

Lab office, 263
Lab Office field, 103
Language-dependent description, 48
Layers, 80
Lifecycle, 28
   document, 28
Local Object button, 222
Logging into SAP PLM 7.02 DMS, 178
Long-term retention, 37

M

Material master, 182
MaxCacheSize, 123
ME10, 210
Measurement tools, 80
Medusa, 210
Microsoft Office, 257
Microsoft Office integration, 109
Microsoft Windows Explorer, 166
Microsoft Word, 106
Microstation, 210
MIL-RII Ð TRIFF, 79
MIME type field, 107
Multiple languages, 34
Multiple original files, 58
Multi-step workflow definition, 218
My Objects feature, 188

N

Neutral file, 263
Neutral format, 37
New version
   create, 55

Non-SAP DMS authorization object, 145
Number Assignment, 89
Number Exit, 90
Number ranges, 84
   external, 84
   internal, 84

O

Object Check, 93
Object link, 50, 55, 141, 182, 263
Object linking, 86
Object Links, 49
Object Links tab, 66
Object Navigator, 193
Object oriented programming (OOP), 236
Object type
   DRAW, 223
Office integration, 238, 249
Organizational change management, 39
Original file, 52, 121, 238, 243, 264
   add, 46
   change, 56
   check in, 46, 58
   copy, 71
   display, 59
Originals Processing tab, 184
Override of ACL via authorization object, 151
Owner, 27

P

PCT, PICT, 79
PCX, 79
PDF, 37
Personal Object Work List, 194
PNG, 79
Portal iViews, 155
Prev. 1-6, 94
Processed Documents button, 53
Process route, 186, 204, 264
Product Structure Browser, 43, 72
Pro/Engineer, 210

Profile key, 116
Program
 MCDOKDEL, 69
Program exit, 94
Project resources, 22
Project type authorization, 140
Prototype, 26
PS, 79

R

RAS, 79
Redline and markup, 264
Redlining of images, 80
Registry settings, 167
Released, 31, 217
Release Flag, 70, 93
Release Level, 28
Rename temporary file, 107
Report
 MCDOKDEL, 114
Reset check-out, 71
Responsible lab office, 27
Retention period, 36
Review the change history, 61
Revision, 33, 264
Revision level, 70, 104
Rev. Lev. Assgmt., 89
Right hemisphere, 264
Roles, 30

S

SAP application consultant, 22
SAP Basis/IT infrastructure resources, 22
SAP Business Workplace, 232
SAP Classification System, 47
SAP DMS, 19
 availability, 23
 BAdIs and user exits, 257
 benefits, 20
 CAD system, 256
 configuring, 83, 254
 frontend, 155, 255
 future outlook, 257

SAP DMS (Cont.)
 portal iView, 175
 project complexity, 21
 project questions, 254
 security, 255
 step-by-step instructions, 254
 transactions, 43
SAP DMS Project, 254
SAP Easy DMS, 155, 164, 237
 configuration, 166
 implementing, 175
 installation, 166
SAP Easy DMS, 264
SAP ECC 6.0, 23
SAP Enhancements, 236
SAP GUI, 155, 178
SAP IMG configuration items, 198
SAP Knowledge Provider, 37
SAP MaxDB, 121
SAP NetWeaver Business Client, 178
SAP NetWeaver Process Integration, 37
SAP PLM 7.0, 177
SAP PLM 7.01, 23, 78, 126, 151, 240, 252
SAP PLM 7.02, 23, 177, 256
 Web UI Features, 188, 197
SAP Visual Enterprise, 214
 Author, 215
 Generator, 78, 129, 134, 215
 Viewer, 78, 130, 215, 264
Searching, 171
Search requirements, 27
Secure storage, 47, 253
Security, 44, 135
Security requirements, 30, 135
Sending notifications, 28
Sequence of sources, 69
Set Up Web Documents, 157
Side Panel, 192
Sign.Strat., 94
Simple document approval, 256
Simple Search feature, 189
Solid Edge, 210
SolidWorks, 210
Stamping functionality, 238, 249
Standard attributes, 27
Standard SAP authorization object, 137

Index

Start Authorization checkbox, 107
Start conditions, 224
Start processing for documents, 112
Status Change, 89
Status-dependent authorization, 138
Status log, 70, 264
Status network, 44, 55, 70, 86, 92, 264
  display, 59
  graphic, 97
Status Type, 94
Steps to configuration, 84
Stereolithography (STL), 79
Storing files, 27
Superior Document, 69, 264
System architecture, 131

T

Technology behind WebDocuments, 156
Templates for original files, 110
Terminating events tab, 227
Thumbnail, 114
TIF, 37, 79
Training, 39
Transaction
  CC04, 43, 72
  CDESK, 211
  Change Document, 52
  CL02, 100
  CL30N, 43, 75
  Class Maintenance, 100
  CSADMIN, 122
  CV01N, 43, 69, 246
  CV02N, 43, 53, 246
  CV03N, 43, 59, 246
  CV04N, 43, 63, 77, 112, 115, 171, 239, 247
  CV11, 71
  CVI8, 76
  CVI9, 77
  Display Document, 59
  Distribution Log, 77
  LPD_CUST, 202

Transaction (Cont.)
  OACO, 122
  OACT, 122
  PFTC, 218
  SBWP, 232
  SCMSCA, 124
  SCMSHO, 124
  SCMSIP, 124
  SCMSMO, 122
  SE18, 235
  SE38, 69, 114
  SE80, 156
  SMOD, 236
  SPRO, 84
  Start Document Distribution, 76
  SWU3, 218
Transport request, 225
TREX, 34, 126, 255, 263
Triggering event, 223
TXT, 79

U

UG NX, 214
Unigraphics, 210
URL, 239, 248
Use KPro, 89
User exit, 235, 251, 257
  CV000001, 236, 251
  CV110001, 251
  CVDI0001, 251
  CVDI0002, 251
  CVDI0003, 251
  CVDI0004, 251
  CVDI0005, 251
  CVDI0006, 251
  CVDI0007, 251
  CVDI0008, 251
  CVDI0009, 251
  CVDI0010, 251
  CVDI0011, 251
  CVDI0020, 251
  CVDS0001, 251
Using filters, 174

V

Valid from, 264
Version, 33
Version Assgmt., 89
Vers. No. Incr., 90
Viewer application, 202
Virtual Reality Modeling Language (WRL), 79

W

WebDocuments, 155
  configuration, 158
WebDocuments frontend, 155, 160
WebUI, 256
  Inbox, 197

White list setup, 205
Wide area network capability, 132
Workflow
  adding tasks, 225
  Builder, 223
  definition, 218
  notification, 217
  scenario, 217
Workflow Task
  Object Type/Object ID, 94
Workstation application, 105, 107, 116, 200, 264

Y

"You can also" link, 192, 202

Interested in reading more?

Please visit our website for all new
book and e-book releases from SAP PRESS.

www.sap-press.com